KILLARNEY TO –THE IVERAG
A WALKING GUIDE

ADRIAN HENDROFF is a qualified mountain guide and a member of the Outdoor Writers and Photographers Guild. His articles and photographs have been widely published. He has explored the mountains of Scotland, Wales, England, Romania, Iceland, the European Alps and the Dolomites, but he thinks of the Irish mountains as home. His previous books include *From High Places: A Journey Through Ireland's Great Mountains* (2010), *The Dingle, Iveragh & Beara Peninsulas: A Walking Guide* (2011) and *Donegal, Sligo & Leitrim: Mountain & Coastal Hillwalks* (2012).

Visit Adrian's website at: www.adrianhendroff.com

You can also keep up to date at:

- www.facebook.com/adrianhendroff.exploreirelandsmountains and
- www.twitter.com/exp_ireland_mtn

Looking toward Knocknadobar from the Beentee ridge.

Disclaimer

Acknowledgements

There are several people whose encouragement, participation and support were invaluable during the making of this guidebook, and to whom I owe a huge debt of gratitude.

In particular, I would like to thank Tanya and Una, for the proof-reading and support. Thanks also to The Collins Press for your patience and continued support in my work, and for your expertise as always.

For your kindness, welcome and hospitality I should thank: Maureen and John, Maureen and Noel, Brendan Kelliher and Christina Evans.

I would like to acknowledge the following for a number of reasons: Gerry Christie, Gerard Sheehy, John Cronin, Nessa O'Shaughnessy, Peter Corless, Peter van der Burgt, Sean O'Donoghue and Tanya Oliver. Also to: Colin and Hannah from Glenbeigh; Brid, Anne, Julie and Charlie from Killarney; Richard, Ricky, Sarah and Ronaz from Ennis; Richard from Cheshire; Paddy, Lorcan, Maria and Aoife from Tralee; Sheila, Pat and Margaret from the Black Valley; Bridgette from Calw; Renee from Berlin; Peter, Susie, Christine, Katherine and gang; Jonathan from Bavaria; Anita of Cahersiveen; Michael, Heather and Lewis from Scotland.

For my friends, thank you for your friendship: Alan and Margaret Tees, Alun Richardson, Barry Speight, Charles O'Byrne, Colin Soosay, Conor O'Hagan, Conor Murphy, Gerry McVeigh, Iain Miller, John Noble, Martin McCormack, Niamh Gaffney, Oisin Reid, Pat Falvey, Paul & Bairbre Duffy, Ray Chambers, Raymond and Suzanne Cummins, Richie Casey, Ronan Colgan, Stephen Bender, Steve Brown, Teena Gates and Tim McSweeney. Also in remembrance and respect to my friends: Ian McKeever RIP and Joss Lynam RIP.

Finally to Grandpa, Kay and Una, a huge thanks for your love, patience and continuous support.

For those I may have forgotten to mention, please accept my apology in advance, as this is merely an oversight.

Muckross Lake, with Eagles Nest and Shehy Mountain in the background.

KILLARNEY to VALENTIA ISLAND –THE IVERAGH PENINSULA:
A WALKING GUIDE

ADRIAN HENDROFF

The Collins Press

For James, Aaron, Emma and baby Anna

FIRST PUBLISHED IN 2015 BY
The Collins Press
West Link Park
Doughcloyne
Wilton
Cork

A CIP record for this book is available from the British Library.

Paperback ISBN: 978-1-84889-232-3

Design and typesetting by Fairways Design

Typeset in Myriad Pro

Printed in Poland by Białostockie Zakłady Graficzne SA

Contents

Route Location Map

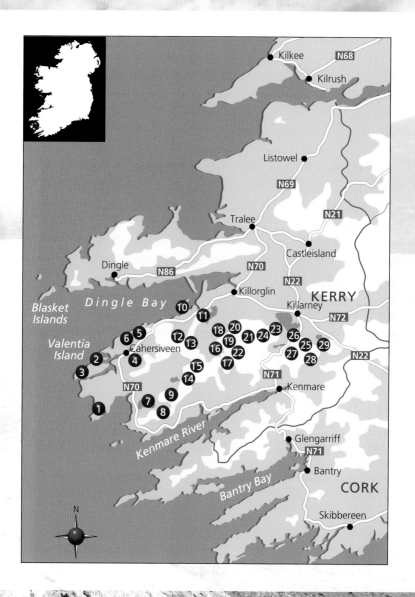

Quick Reference Route Table

No.	Walk Name	Category
1	Bolus and Ducalla Heads	
	Normal route	Coastal Path and Hillwalk
	Long variation	Coastal Path and Hillwalk
2	Geokaun	Coastal Path
3	Bray Head	Coastal Path
4	Beentee Loop	Mountain Path and Hillwalk
5	Knocknadobar from Roads	Hillwalk
6	Knocknadobar via Stations of the Cross	Mountain Path and Hillwalk
7	Lough Currane Circuit	Mountain Path and Hillwalk
8	Eagles Hill and Mullaghbeg	Hillwalk
9	Coomcallee Circuit	Hillwalk
10	Rossbeigh Strand	Coastal Walk
11	Seefin Loop	Mountain Path and Hillwalk
12	Coomasaharn Horseshoe	
	Normal route	Hillwalk
	Extended variation	Hillwalk
13	Coomaclarig and Curravaha Horseshoe	
	Normal route	Hillwalk
	Short variation	Hillwalk
14	Coomnacronia, Knockmoyle and Knocknagantee	Hillwalk
15	The Cloon Horseshoe	Hillwalk
16	Gearhameen Circuit	Hillwalk
17	Knocklomena–Boughil Ridge	Hillwalk
18	The Coomloughra Horseshoe	Hillwalk
19	Carrauntoohil via O'Shea's Gully	Hillwalk
20	Coomloughra Lakes via The Hydro Road	Mountain Path and Low-level Hillwalk, optional Scramble
21	The Reeks Ridge	
	Normal route	Hillwalk and Scramble
	Cnoc an Chuillin variation	Hillwalk and Scramble
22	Lough Acoose to Kate Kearney's Cottage	
	Normal route	Mountain Path and Hillwalk
	Including Brassel Mountain	Mountain Path and Hillwalk
23	Tomies, Shehy and Purple Mountain	Hillwalk
24	Strickeen, The Eastern Reeks and Drishana	Hillwalk
25	Torc Mountain	Mountain Path and Hillwalk
26	Muckross Lake Loop	Forest and Lake Walk
27	Old Kenmare Road	
	Galway's Bridge to Kenmare	Mountain Path
	Torc Waterfall to Kenmare	Mountain Path
28	Mangerton Mountain and Stoompa	
	Normal route	Hillwalk
	Stoompa variation	Hillwalk
29	Bennaunmore and Crohane	Hillwalk

Torc Waterfall

Introduction

And there I asked beneath a lonely cloud
Of strange delight, with one bird singing loud,
What change you'd wrought in graveyard, rock and sea,
This new wild paradise to wake for me ….
Yet knew no more than knew those merry sins
Had built this stack of thigh-bones, jaws and shins.

– John Millington Synge ('In Kerry')

Synge calls it a 'wild paradise' and its mountains a 'stack of thigh-bones, jaws and shins'. I couldn't agree more, having enjoyed a decade of exploring the mountains in this irresistible corner of Ireland.

It is astonishing to think that during the Devonian Period, 350 to 410 million years ago, this region was an arid, hot and low-lying alluvial plain. Sediments of substantial thickness were deposited by southward-flowing seasonal rivers. These sedimentary layers formed the distinctive reddish or purplish Old Red Sandstone rock that is common to the region today.

Chaos followed. A mountain-building episode 280 to 340 million years ago resulted in tectonic forces compressing and thrusting up layers of rock in east–west folds. The mountains of Kerry were born during this Hercynian or Variscan orogeny.

The peaks of the Iveragh Peninsula were then of Alpine proportions. However, erosion, hard weathering and glaciations over the past 280 million years have gnawed away at these giant peaks, trimming them to their present size. The hard sandstone cores resisted erosion and their defiance formed the sandstone rock ridges, slabs and ribs that today make up most of the highlands of this peninsula.

Ice then became the master sculptor from about 2 million years ago on more than one occasion. Monstrous tongues of ice pushed their way northwards and north-westwards across these peninsulas carving deep, steep-sided and lake-filled corries; forming hanging valleys; dragging large boulders and depositing moraine sediments along the valley floors.

We have much for which to thank this epoch of geological landscape building as we walk the rugged peaks, dramatic ridges, captivating valleys and glittering lakes of the Iveragh Peninsula today.

A spine of mountains punches the Iveragh skyline, dominating the view inland from a coastal ring road that weaves its way along the fringes of the peninsula. It is much larger than its two neighbouring peninsulas, Dingle and Beara, which encapsulate it to the north and south respectively. A series of mountains run riot along the length of Iveragh, forming a backbone of approximately 55km (34 miles): from its western tip at Farraniaragh Mountain to a range of hills further inland around the Mangerton massif.

Nine of the ten highest summits in Ireland, all of which are over 914m (3,000ft), sit on the lofty heights of the MacGillycuddy's Reeks. The peninsula also contains a whopping 66 Vandeleur-Lynam summits, all of these over 600m with a 15m prominence: 21 in the Dunkerrons, 4 in Iveragh north-west, 9 in Glenbeigh, 4 in the Purple Mountain range, 8 in the Mangerton range and 20 in the MacGillycuddy's Reeks.

The Kerry Way, one of Ireland's best known long-distance walking trails, starts and ends in Killarney and covers 214km (133 miles) of quiet country roads, ancient field paths, covered woodland, open moorland, scenic hillside and lonely mountain passes. The total ascent over the entire Kerry Way is a staggering 5,310m (17,421ft) and the entire trail takes an estimated nine days to complete.

The Ring of Kerry, a world-famous tourist driving route and now marketed as part of the Wild Atlantic Way, runs for nearly 179km (111 miles) along Iveragh's coastline, covering the towns of Killarney, Killorglin, Glenbeigh, Kells, Cahersiveen, Waterville, Portmagee, Ballinskelligs, Caherdaniel, Sneem and Kenmare. The Skellig Ring drive, also part of the Wild Atlantic Way, has added more distance to the coastal ring road and takes in Valentia Island, Portmagee, St Finian's Bay and Ballinskelligs.

Mountains, walking trails and roads apart, the Iveragh landscape exhibits a raw and stunning beauty, from the hundreds of lakes which fill its secluded corries to the spectacular cliffs that line its coast. There is no better way to explore this beautiful and timeless landscape than on foot.

There is too much to write about the Iveragh Peninsula to pack into an introduction, so allow me to reveal its secrets in a collection of 29 carefully selected walking routes. These range from easy to difficult routes of various grades, and last from a few hours to a full day. The routes are designed to cover the length of the peninsula in a general west-to-east direction and include sections of the Kerry Way, beach strolls, woodland trails, coastal paths, island walks, lake circuits, scenic hill walks, classic mountain circuits and some scrambling opportunities. Route selection has been tailored to be different from previous or existing guidebooks and a range of variations and extensions are also given. All routes have been checked in 2013 and 2014, with access foremost in mind. However, as access may be withdrawn at any time, if you do encounter any problems any of the routes described in this book, please contact the publisher and me so we can address the issue in future editions.

I genuinely hope that this guidebook will lead to many great mountain days of your own in this exhilarating corner of Ireland. For every one walk in this guidebook, I can think of another half-dozen variations – so finishing all the routes it is not necessarily the end of exploration.

The majority of these routes are quiet: for most of the time you will not encounter anyone else. So revel in the freedom of the Iveragh hills, escape from an increasingly rushed and weary world, and enjoy the peace and comfort it brings.

Using This Book

Maps

The maps in this guidebook are approximate representations of the routes only. For all routes in this guidebook, the use of detailed maps is imperative. All maps listed below are Ordnance Survey Ireland (OSi) Discovery Series 1:50,000 unless otherwise stated. Laminated versions are recommended for durability in wind and rain. Note that 1:50,000 OSi maps do not show cliffs, crags, boulder fields or areas of scree. Also, forestry, tracks and waymarked trails may also change from time to time, so it is useful to get the latest edition. (As of 2015, this is the 4th edition for 1:50,000 maps.)

The following 1:50,000 maps are required for this guidebook:

- OSi Sheet 83: **Routes 1–9, 12**
- OSi Sheet 78: **Routes 10–28**
- OSi Sheet 79: **Routes 28–29**

There are also even more detailed maps of the MacGillycuddy's Reeks and Killarney National Park suited for use for Routes 16–28 of this guidebook. Note that these are of a different scale to the 1:50,000 maps and also have different contour intervals and colouring schemes.

- OSi 1:25,000 Adventure Series: *MacGillycuddy's Reeks and Killarney National Park*, Preliminary ed. 2014. Note: the Adventure Series map is a new version of the older set of maps (I) OSi 1:25,000 *MacGillycuddy's Reeks Weatherproof*, 2nd ed. (II) OSi 1:25,000 *Killarney National Park*, 2nd ed.
- Harvey Superwalker 1:30,000 *MacGillycuddy's Reeks and Killarney National Park*, 2006. This map also shows tracks and cliffs in detail and a summit enlargement of Carrauntoohil at 1:15,000.

Grid References

Grid references (e.g. **V 504**$_{47}$ **843**$_{76}$) provided in this book should help you plan a route and upload it to your GPS or to use your GPS to check a grid reference on the mountain. Set your GPS to use the Irish Grid (IG). Note that GPS units are precise to 5 digits, whereas a 3-digit precision will usually suffice using map and compass, and hence these are in **bold**.

Walking Times

Walking times in this book are calculated based on individual speeds of 3 to 4km per hour. One minute has also been added for every 10m of ascent, so for example if a height gain of 300m is the case, then 30 minutes would be added to the total walking time. So a 6km route with a total of 300m ascent will take 2 to 2½ hours. In some routes, I have also added time for the difficulty of terrain. These are: Route 15 (The Cloon Horseshoe), Route 18 (The Coomloughra Horseshoe), Route 21 (The Reeks Ridge) and Route 29 (Bennaunmore and Crohane).

Note that the 'Time' stated in the routes of this guidebook does not include the additional time required for stops, lunch, photography, etc.

Metric and imperial units are given for road approaches (as some vehicles may be still using miles), total distance, total ascent and mountain heights. However, walking distances are given in metric to conform to OSi maps.

Walk Grades

Walks in this book are graded 1 to 5 based on *level of difficulty*, with 1 being the easiest and 5 the hardest.

None of the routes involves any technical mountaineering or rock climbing. However, note that in winter under snow and ice conditions, all Grade 4 and 5 routes become a serious mountaineering venture requiring the use of winter mountaineering skills, crampons and ice axes. All routes with the exception of Grade 1 walks require three- to four-season hillwalking boots.

Grade 1:   Suited for beginners or families with children, these routes are on well-graded or constructed paths with good and firm underfoot conditions. There are little to no navigational difficulties as the routes are generally easy or signposted throughout. Grade 1 routes involve minimal amount of total vertical ascent.

Grade 2:   Suited for beginners with some hillwalking experience, these routes are generally on formal paths or well-graded, constructed paths with good underfoot conditions. However, there may be some sections of open countryside or slightly rougher ground. The routes are generally signposted, but there may be sections with no signs and require basic navigational skills. Grade 2 routes involve up to 500m of total vertical ascent.

Grade 2/3: Grade 2 routes with over 15km of total distance fall into this category.

Grade 3: Previous hillwalking experience is required. There may be some formal and signposted paths but generally these routes involve informal paths and rougher ground of open mountainside. There may be some sections of rocky and uneven ground, and small sections of cliffs and moderately steep ground. As they are generally not signed, good navigational skills in all weather conditions are required. Grade 3 routes involve from 500m to 800m of total vertical ascent.

Grade 4: Suited for those with solid hillwalking experience. Paths are generally informal and underfoot conditions are rough. There may be prolonged sections of rocky and uneven ground. Solid mountain navigation skills are required to cope with all weather conditions. The ability to deal with hazards such as cliffs, small sections of scree and steep ground is required. Grade 4 routes involve from 800m to 1,000m of total vertical ascent.

Grade 5: Suited for those with solid hillwalking experience. Paths are generally informal and underfoot conditions are rough. There may be prolonged sections of rocky and uneven ground. Solid mountain navigation skills are required to cope with all weather conditions. The ability to deal with hazards such as cliffs, small sections of scree and steep ground is required. There are sections of considerable exposure and where basic scrambling skills are required. Grade 5 routes are strenuous and involve over 1,000m of total vertical ascent.

Access

All land in the Republic of Ireland is owned privately or by the State, with no legal right of entry to the land. When you hear the term 'commonage' it implies that the private property is held in common by a number of joint owners.

Access to upland and mountain areas has traditionally been granted out of the goodwill, permission and discretion of landowners. It is normally good practice to strike up a friendly conversation with a farmer or landowner, and if there is any doubt about access, do ask them. If you are asked to leave, please do so politely and without argument or aggravating the situation.

Note also the provisions of the Occupiers Liability Act 1995 contain a definition that reduces the landowner's duty of care to hillwalkers. This act contains a category of 'recreational users' who, when they enter farmland, are responsible for their own safety. This has significantly reduced the possibility of successful legal claims against landowners by hillwalkers.

Always use gates and stiles where available. If a gate is closed, close it after entering. If it is open, leave it open. If you cannot open a closed gate to enter, go over at its hinge with care. Take care not to damage any gates, stiles or fences.

When parking, be considerate not to block any gates, farm access lanes or forest entrances as local residents, farm machinery and emergency services may need access at all times.

Note that landowners generally do not approve of dogs being brought on their property, and this includes their land on the open hillside.

Mountain Safety

1. Get a detailed weather forecast. Useful sources of information are www.met.ie, www.mountain-forecast.com and www.yr.no

2. There is a temperature drop of 2 to 3 °C for every 300m of ascent. If it is a pleasant morning at sea level it could be cold on the summit of Carrauntoohil. The wind is around 25 per cent stronger at 500m as it is at sea level. Wind velocities at a col are higher and wind effects could be strong on an exposed ridge.

3. In case of emergency call 999/112 and ask for 'Mountain Rescue'. Before dialling, it helps to be ready to give a grid location of your position.

4. Keep well away from cliff edges. Be cautious of wet or slippery rock and holes in the ground on vegetated slopes. Take your time traversing a boulder field, descending a scree slope and during scrambling.

5. Rivers, marked as 'thick' blue lines on OSi maps, can sometimes be little streams. Similarly, some streams, marked as 'thin' blue lines, can be wide rivers in reality. Remember also that rivers or streams in flood are dangerous and water levels can rise *very* quickly after or during wet days. Always cross rivers with boots on – remove your socks to keep them dry, use a plastic liner inside your boots to cross, use a towel to dry your feet and boots after, and then put your dry socks back on. Avoid river crossings early in the day. If you cannot cross a river in spate, head upstream to increase your chances in crossing. Do not cross rivers at a bend: rather, cross on a straight.

6. Ensure that you and your clothing and equipment are up to the task, and know the limitations of both. Winter conditions require specialised gear.

7. Be aware of the daylight hours over the time of year. Most accidents happen during descent or near the end of the day. Carry enough emergency equipment (e.g. a head torch, survival shelter and spare batteries) should an injury occur and you need to stop moving.

8. It is recommended not to walk alone, except in areas where there are other people around. Leave word with someone responsible.

9. Do not leave any valuables in cars. Keep all things in the boot and out of sight to avoid unwanted attention.

10. Carry a fully charged mobile phone, but keep it well away from the compass as its needle is affected by metal.

11. Do not solely rely on the use of GPS. Map and compass skills are imperative.

12. Landowners, especially farmers, move their livestock such as cattle from field to field, and up to higher ground, especially in the summer. Be wary of bulls in fields and cows that are protecting newborn calves: avoid crossing such fields and go another way. If you find yourself in a field of suddenly wary cattle, do not panic and move away calmly without making any sudden noises. The cows may leave you alone if they think you pose no threat.

13. Keep in mind the deer-rutting season from mid September to end October. Stay well away from stags and deer during this time.

TIP: I recommend the use of a plastic tube about 50cm long, slit in half along its length. This helps crossing barbed-wire fences and also prevents damage to them.

Useful Contacts

Emergencies Dial 999 or 112 for emergency services, including mountain rescue and coastguard.

Weather LoCall 1550 123850 for a detailed 5 day Munster forecast using the Met Éireann Weatherdial service.

Maps All walking maps for the Iveragh Peninsula may be purchased from www.osi.ie or www.harveymaps.co.uk

Access and Training Mountaineering Ireland, the representative body for walkers and climbers in Ireland, works to secure continued access and to provide walkers and climbers the opportunity to improve their skills. Tel: +353 (0)1 6251115; www.mountaineering.ie

Hillwalking Resource www.mountainviews.ie is a great hillwalking resource and provides mountain lists, comments and information.

Tourist Information For tourist information and information, visit www.ringofkerrytourism.com Detailed information on the long distance walking trail of the Kerry Way and other National Waymarked Loops may also be found on www.irishtrails.ie or www.kerryway.com

Killarney National Park For information on the park, its history, landscape and walking trails Tel: +353 (0)64 6631440, www.killarneynationalpark.ie

Transport For intercity train services contact Irish Rail on LoCall 1850 366 222 (or +353 (0)1 8366222 from outside Rep. of Ireland); www.irishrail.ie; For intercity bus services contact Bus Éireann on Tel: +353 (0) 21 4508188 (Cork), +353 (0)64 66 30011 (Killarney), +353 (0)66 7164700 (Tralee), +353 (0)61 474311 (Shannon Airport); www.buseireann.ie; Taxis: Euro Taxis Killarney +353(0)64 6637676, www.eurotaxiskillarney.com; O'Grady's Cabs (Waterville) +353 (0)87 2230586, www.ogradyswaterville.com

On top of O'Shea's Gully in winter, with Cummeenoughter Lough below (Route 19)

ROUTE 1:
Bolus and Ducalla Heads

An invigorating walk along a headland with stunning cliff scenery and sweeping coastal panoramas.

Normal Route
Grade: 2
Distance: 10km (6¼ miles)
Ascent: 430m (1,411ft)
Time   3¼–4 hours
Map: OSi 1:50,000 Sheet 83

Long variation
Grade: 2/3
Distance: 21km (13 miles)
Ascent: 530m (1,739ft)
Time   6½–8 hours
Map: OSi 1:50,000 Sheet 83

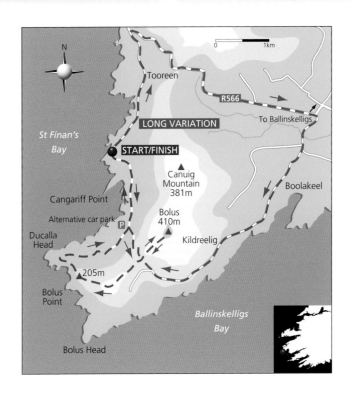

Normal Route

Start/finish: Leave the R566 at a bend in the townland of Killonecaha. Turn into a minor road toward Allagheemore which is signposted 'Bolus Head' and 'Trailhead'. It is best approached from Ballinskelligs, as the R566 from Portmagee is narrow and twisty, with steep inclines and declines. Continue along the minor road for around 2.75km (1¾ miles) to park at **V 388**₅₀ **650**₄₀ by a monument. There are also parking spaces for two cars at a lay-by around 1.5km (1 mile) further at **V 391**₇₃ **636**₉₈, which reduces the road-walk by around 3km.

Bolus Head is the tip of the beak of headland separating Saint Finan's Bay and Ballinskelligs Bay around 20km (12½ miles) from Waterville. Saint Finan's Bay is named after an Irish monk who lived for a time on the Skelligs in the seventh century and who crossed the bay regularly to celebrate Mass at his church on the mainland. Ballinskelligs is part of the beautiful coastal drive of the Skellig Ring between Waterville and Valentia Island. In Irish, *Baile an Sceilge* means 'homestead of the rocks', taken from the jagged rocks of Skellig Michael (*Sceilg Mhichíl*, 'Michael's rock') and Little Skellig (*Sceilg Bheag*, 'little rock') off the coast. This route explores the headland between the two bays, taking in the magnificent sea-cliff and coastal scenery between Bolus Head and Ducalla Head. There are good mountain trails and solid tarmac throughout, except for an optional section to summit Bolus Hill (410m/1,345ft). A longer variation is also outlined which visits the eastern side of Bolus.

Route Description

The normal route starts from the car park at the monument to the US naval plane *Liberator*, which crashed off the Skelligs coast in 1944. Continue southward along the road for around 1.5km to reach a fork. There is a lay-by to the right. The entire route, except for the ascent of Bolus Hill, is signposted by National Loop markers.

The barracks at Bolus Head with Bolus Hill in the background.

Take a left at the fork and follow the lane uphill, passing some houses, to reach a metal gate with a ladder stile. Continue uphill past the last house on the left to meet another metal gate with a ladder stile. A grassy

Ducalla Head.

track leads uphill to reach a saddle below Bolus Hill. A few houses dot the landscape on either side of the saddle.

Turn left here to follow an intermittent path uphill, keeping a fence on the right. Gorse on the slopes can be prickly at times, but this gives way to heather as height is gained. Cross the fence at the end of path and continue until reaching a trig pillar on Bolus Hill.

Bolus Hill rewards the visitor with fabulous 360-degree views, with sweeping vistas of Saint Finan's Bay and Ballinskelligs Bay. The view extends to a circular panorama of rolling hills, green plains, sandy beaches, a blue lake and brown mountains from the striated green blade of Puffin Island to Hog's Head.

Retrace steps from Bolus Hill back down to the saddle. During the descent, an old military barracks can be seen at the end of a broad, green ridge. To the right of the barracks, and a few miles out to sea, is the jagged profile of the Skellig Islands.

Cross a ladder stile at the saddle and follow a broad track, keeping a fence to the left. The track leads gradually uphill and over another stile by the ruins of the old barracks. Pass the barracks on the left, and then a small concrete hut.

Veer right and follow a path downhill keeping a fence and the sea to your left to reach the ruins of an old stone hut at point 205m. This is the clifftop above Bolus Point with good views of the coastline along Saint Finan's Bay to the north.

Follow loop markers, and with the sea to your left, continue in the direction of Ducalla Head. Just after passing point 130m, veer left to descend slightly along the clifftop. Just after a notch, look southward at **V 379**69 **630**38 along the coastline toward Bolus Point at some impressive cliffs and a cove below. You may want to linger here and watch the waves crashing on the rocks below, and choughs, fulmars and herring gulls in full flight.

From here, retrace steps back to the loop marker and follow it to the last signpost where the path veers right. This is at **V 378**57 **630**70 and before the slope flattens at point 71m near Ducalla Head. There are fine views of the low cliffs at Ducalla Head, and Puffin Island and the Skelligs out to sea.

Turn right at the last marker post and an angular descent eastwards beckons. The loop soon crosses a stream after around 700m, then zigzags along a line of ditches before rising gently to meet a ladder stile at **V 388**37 **632**61 by a metal gate. Cross the stile and follow the road for around 2km back to the car park at the start.

Long Variation

Start/finish: Leave the R566 at a bend just after Ballinskelligs village and take the minor road towards Boolakeel (*Baile Ui Chuill*) or Kildreelig (*Cill Rialaigh*). Go over Ballinskelligs Bridge and ignore a junction on the right after around 750m (½ mile). Take a right at a fork soon after and continue for another 1.75km (1 mile) to park at a lay-by near a quarry at **V 415**00 **636**87 where there are spaces for 2 cars. You may also leave a second car at either of the start points of the normal route to reduce the road-walk at the end by 10km to 11.5km.

Route Description

From the quarry or the Artist Retreat Village, walk uphill toward Kildreelig on a narrow surfaced road with good seaward views to the left. Pass some ruined buildings, stone-walled fields and the site of an old oratory and cross slabs. The road passes a house and quarry on the right and above bracken-covered slopes falling steeply into the sea.

Continue uphill on tarmac to reach a lay-by on right. There is an 'End of route – please turn back now' sign at **V 399**27 **626**88 – out of courtesy, please do not park here. A network of stone-walled fields can be seen on seaward slopes, and then the road bends, passing two houses followed by an abandoned zinc-roofed building on the left.

Leave the road and turn right there at **V 394**89 **628**75 on a grassy track uphill to reach a metal gate. There are electric lines to the left of the track, which eventually leads to a metal gate with a ladder stile on the left at the saddle. Turn right here for Bolus Hill (as per the normal route), retrace steps back to the saddle, and then continue (as per the normal route) toward the car park by the Liberator Monument via the barracks and Ducalla Head. From the car park, follow the minor road northward past Tooreen until meeting the R566. Turn right and follow the R566 for some 4.5km to the junction for Boolakeel and Kildreelig. Turn right there and follow the road the way you came back to the start point at the quarry.

ROUTE 2:
Geokaun

This is a walk to suit all abilities with minimal ascent and stupendous views of west Iveragh and Valentia Island.

Grade:	1
Distance:	3.5km (2¼ miles)
Ascent:	100m (328ft)
Time:	1–1½ hours
Map:	OSi 1:50,000 Sheet 83

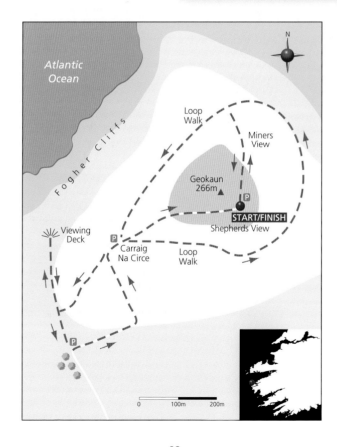

Start/finish: There are signs for Geokaun at most junctions on Valentia Island. However, here are the two most straightforward ways to reach the Mountain Park. **(A)** If accessing Valentia Island by ferry from Reenard Point, turn right at the quay upon exiting the ferry. Drive through Knightstown village until reaching a Y-junction at a church. Take a right there and continue for 2.75km (1¾ miles). Pass a wooded area and take a sharp left, followed by the next right. Continue on this road for around 1.6km (1 mile). The entrance to Geokaun Mountain will be on the right. **(B)** If accessing Valentia Island by the Maurice O'Neill Memorial Bridge at Portmagee, turn left at the top of the road after the bridge. Continue for around 1.6km (1 mile) and turn right at a junction by Foilhomurrin Bay. Follow the narrow road for around 4.3km (2¾ miles) to reach the entrance for Geokaun Mountain on your left just before a wooded area. There is an entrance fee of €5 per car/family or €2 per pedestrian/cyclist and it is useful to have exact coins available. Ignore intermediate car parks at Fogher Cliffs and Carraig na Circe. Drive up to the top of the mountain road and park there by a transmission mast.

On the rocks by the sea near Valentia Radio Station at Coosadillisk below to the north is a 385-million-year-old fossil trackway. The trackway is a series of footprints of a tetrapod, a large amphibian that walked on soft sediments and its footprints are now preserved in the rock as shallow impressions. The car park is practically at the summit of Geokaun, at 266m (873ft), the highest point on Valentia Island. Like the tetrapod, all that remains is to enjoy the spectacular views by following a modern trackway that circumnavigates it.

Route Description

Fogher cliffs.

From car park at the top, follow the signposted 'Miners View' track a short distance until reaching some information panels on rock slabs. There are good views down to Doulus Bay and the north-east of the island from here, including the 1914 Valentia Radio Station building and the 1841 lighthouse near Murreagh Point.

Descend northward down a grassy slope to meet a firm path just below. Turn left on the path and with the sea to your right continue until reaching the viewing area at Carraig na Circe dominated by more information panels. There are fine views down to the fishing village of

The hills of Kerry bathed in evening light behind Valentia Harbour, Doulus Bay and Lough Kay, as seen from the summit slopes of Geokaun.

Portmagee (*An Caladh*, 'the quay') and along the length of Valentia Island toward Bray Head. The Skelligs and Great Blasket Island can also be seen out to sea.

Not far from here, at Culloo, legend has it that St Brendan the Navigator scaled its sea cliffs in the sixth century to baptise two dying pagans. A holy well and stone crosses sit near this site at *Tobár Olla Bhreanáin*. Interestingly, another navigator also passed over this area: in 1927 Charles Lindberg flew the first solo transatlantic flight from New York to Paris on *The Spirit of St Louis* and was cheered on by James O'Leary who lived beside the well.

The next section of the route leaves the path for a short distance. Walk on grass in the direction of Bray Head toward a slab of pointed rock at **V 382**$_{30}$ **768**$_{65}$. Pass the rock slab and descend a grassy slope in the direction of Bray Head, to meet a track below at **V 381**$_{40}$ **767**$_{45}$. Turn right on the track and continue to reach the Fogher Cliffs viewing deck, passing more information panels on the way. Enjoy the views there toward the cliffs and coastline to the north towards Coosnahorna and Reenadrolaun Point.

> **Note:** If you are not comfortable with going off the path at Carrig na Circe, follow the road down from there. Go around a bend to reach the Fogher Cliffs car park below. Turn right there to meet a track and continue until reaching the viewing deck at the cliffs.

From the viewing deck, walk back out on the track to reach a double gate by the car park. Turn left at the road, following signs for 'Peak', 'Looped walk' and 'Viewing points'. The road goes quite steeply uphill before reaching the Carraig na Circe viewing area.

The road bends right after passing Carraig na Circe. A few metres after, leave the road by turning right and follow the sign for 'Loop Walk 1 mile'. A path circumnavigates the slopes just below Geokaun Hill, ultimately leading back to the Miners View viewing area at the start.

Simply follow the path, with the long arm of Portmagee Channel initially down to your right. The path then loops around the eastern end of Geokaun to reach a fork at **V 387**44 **769**56. Take the right fork there and continue until reaching the area below Miners View. This is easily the best section of the walk as the panorama to the right down to Valentia Harbour, Lough Kay and Doulus Bay is stupendous. The view is topped off by the impressive Kerry landscape from the cliffs at Doulus Head toward the imposing mound of Knocknadobar and then across to Cahersiveen town and Beentee Hill behind.

The lighthouse also comes into view again, with Beginish Island separated by a channel of water behind it. A collection of smaller islands can be seen behind Beginish – Lamb Island, Black Rock and Church Island. Church Island has its name from the discovery of a medieval monastic site and graveyard excavated by M. J. O'Kelly in 1955 and 1956.

From the area under the Miners View, retrace steps back up the slope and to the car park at the start.

Bray Head

This short, exhilarating walk gives fabulous coastal views and visits dramatic sea cliffs on Valentia Island.

Grade:	2
Distance:	6km (3¾ miles)
Ascent:	260m (853ft)
Time:	2–2½ hours
Map:	OSi 1:50,000 Sheet 83

Start/finish: This is best approached from the Maurice O'Neill Memorial Bridge at Portmagee. Turn left at the top of the road after the bridge. Continue for around 1.6km (1 mile) and turn left at a junction by Foilhomurrin Bay. Continue for around 400m (¼ mile) to a large car park on the left at **V 350**₆₁ **737**₄₂. There is a €2 fee per car to park.

Near the car park is the site where the first undersea transatlantic telegraph cable was laid from the middle to late nineteenth century, connecting Foilhomurrin Bay in Valentia Island to Heart's Content in eastern Newfoundland. On 16 August 1858 the first message sent was, 'Europe and America are united by telegraphy. Glory to God in the highest: on earth, peace and goodwill toward men.' Queen Victoria then sent a congratulatory telegram to President James Buchanan in Pennsylvania. The President responded: 'It is a triumph more glorious, because far more useful to mankind, than was ever won by conqueror on the field of battle.' These messages were followed by a grand salute of 100 guns in New York City. Its streets were decorated with flags, church bells rang, and at night the city was grandly illuminated. The communication time between North America and Europe was reduced from ten days – the time it took to deliver a message by ship – to a matter of hours and minutes.

This route follows National Loop markers throughout and the highlights include a signal tower on the edge of the sea and some towering sea cliffs.

Route Description

The pretty alcove of Foilhomurrin Bay immediately catches the eye at the car park and one will be instantly drawn to look across the channel toward Horse Island, Long Island and the tableland of hills of Kilkeaveragh and Knocknaskereighta behind. The sea cliffs south of Dromgour can be seen to the right of the panorama, along with Puffin Island and the Skelligs further out to sea.

Sea cliffs north of the signal tower at Bray Head. The route to Foiltagarriff skirts along the clifftop.

The two rocky islands of the Skelligs with their needle-like pinnacles were prominently featured in the end sequence of the 1976 German film *Herz aus Glas*, ('Heart of Glass') by Werner Herzog. It was also chosen as a site for the filming of a J. J. Abrams' *Star Wars* film in 2014.

The signal tower at Bray Head

Besides Jedis, the Skelligs have had their fair share of occupants. In AD 490, Duach, the King of West Munster, took refuge on the island when pursued by King Aengus. When Christianity came to Ireland a monastery was founded on Great Skellig's rocky perch in the sixth century: an assemblage of stone huts and oratories, still to be found today. In the eighth and ninth centuries, the island was invaded by Vikings, but despite this, the monastic community survived. From 1821 to 1826, two lighthouses were constructed on the island.

The larger island of Great Skellig, also known as Skellig Michael, is designated as an UNESCO World Heritage Site. Its sharp rocks rise to about 217m (712ft) above the sea. It is a unique bird paradise: Arctic terns with their black cap and red bill, white-headed fulmars, black guillemots, graceful grey-winged kittiwakes with their yellow beak, dark Manx shearwaters, black storm petrels, puffins with their colourful red-and-yellow bill, black-and-white razorbills, and gulls, terns and cormorants are to be found on the island.

The smaller island, Little Skellig, is a noisy gannet colony and now the world's second largest. However, current numbers have dwindled to an estimated 20,000. These white seabirds, with their black-tipped wings, grace every steep ledge on the island, coating its rock like white snowflakes.

Having enjoyed the view, turn left out of the car park and follow the National Loop Walk signpost. Go along a lane and pass a farmhouse on the right. Reach a metal gate and cross a ladder stile slightly further. It should be noted that, although the trail is designated a National Looped Walk, the surrounding hillside is full of cows, which can be anywhere along the track or on the slopes.

Follow a broad track gradually uphill for around 2km to reach the ruins of a stone wall and an old signal tower at **V 330**$_{85}$ **731**$_{33}$. The views to the left out to sea, especially toward the cliffs near Dromgour and Puffin Island improve as height is gained. Three quarters of the way up to the signal tower, on the grassy slopes to the south of the broad track, are the remains of some drystone buildings from early Christian times. These buildings have patterned stones, crosses and other geometric shapes engraved on them.

Bray Head loop marker showing the descent route east of Foiltagarriff, with Valentia Island and Portmagee Channel at sundown.

It is possible to continue a few hundred metres further south-west to point 156m if you wish and then retrace steps back to the tower. The signal tower was built by the English in 1815 in the style of a sixteenth-century Irish tower house. Many such towers were built along the coast for signals to be passed from one to the other in the event of an attack similar to that of the aborted French invasion in 1796. The naval authorities took over the tower in 1907 as a semaphore signal station before it was briefly reoccupied during the Second World War.

It is no surprise, therefore, that the area near the signal tower commands fine coastline views towards the tip of Bray Head, with the jagged outline of the Skelligs dotting the horizon out to sea. In the opposite direction, the vertiginous cliffs of Foiltagarriff impress. Views toward Portmagee are good too, with the Maurice O'Neill Memorial Bridge clearly visible, and the rolling hills behind.

From the signal tower, follow Bray Head Loop markers along a firm path by the grassy clifftop toward point 239m. The ascent is gradual and views of the coastline with its sharp sea cliffs will continuously impress. It is sometimes possible to spot bottlenose dolphin surfacing for air or the outline of a minke whale in the waters below.

The loop signposts veer right just after point 239m and the path leads down a spur to the east of it. Follow the signposts off the grassy and heathery spur, which in summer is covered with windblown bog cotton. The view along the entire length of Valentia Island toward the Fogher cliffs and Geokaun is particularly impressive during the descent.

After around 750m, the path veers right at **V 341**74 **739**53 and descends diagonally downhill. It runs close to a fence and heads back down the slope before running just above the broad track at the start. Follow the signposts back to the car park at the start.

Beentee Loop

A highly enjoyable walking loop following an old Mass path and a ridge to a summit which provides spectacular views of land and sea.

Grade:	2
Distance:	10km (6¼ miles)
Ascent:	380m (1,247ft)
Time:	3¼–4 hours
Map:	OSi 1:50,000 Sheet 83

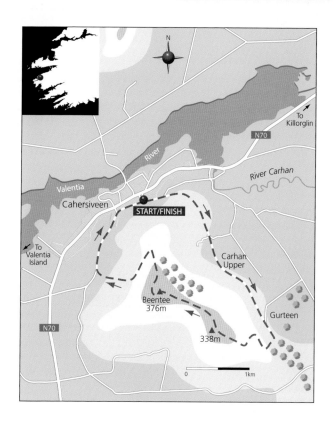

Start/finish: A car park known locally as 'Fairgreen' at **V 473**37 **795**16 at the rear of the Spar Express shop and near a tyre centre and garda station in Cahersiveen.

> O the town it climbs the mountain and looks upon the sea
> And sleeping time or waking time 'tis there I long to be
> > – Sigerson Clifford ('The Boys of Barr na Sráide')

The poet Sigerson Clifford (1913–1985) writes fondly of *Cáthair Saidhbhín*, 'Little Sadhbh's stone ringfort', in his poem named after a street that runs above his beloved boyhood town. The mountain referred to in the poem is the hill overlooking the town, Beentee (376m/1,234ft). A National Loop walking trail has been developed, taking in the foothills to the east of Beentee, then along the ridge running to its summit. This route follows the trail, which is signposted in its entirety, and provides spectacular views of the town, harbour, plains, islands and the surrounding hills.

Route Description

Follow the road at the rear of the car park between the garda station and playground toward a T-junction. Turn left there to follow the trekking man signpost for 'Beentee Loop Walk'. (Note: The OSi 1:50,000 4th edition map labels it as 'Bentee' but Discover Ireland – and the locals – spell it 'Beentee'.) Continue on the road for around 350m to reach a Y-junction. Branch right there and continue uphill, passing some houses and eventually arrive at a ladder stile. Cross the stile and follow a path by a stone wall around the reservoir. Look back here for fine views down to Cahersiveen. Another ladder stile by a ruined building at the other end of the reservoir leads to a track beyond.

The grassy track meanders under the cover of trees and soon passes a wooden bench and a sign for the holy well, *Tobar na mBan Fionn*, at **V 481**71 **794**61 on the left. Continue ahead and cross ladder stiles on either end of a grassy field. Turn right by a metal gate soon after and cross two more stiles. Follow a narrow path, passing a house and a shed on the left before reaching a junction by a boreen at **V 483**87 **788**68.

The hillside toward Beentee away to the right is heavily deforested. Follow the signpost along a grassy path ahead by some fuchsia bushes. Cross a field with a ladder stile on either end and then pass a zinc enclosure on the left. At a fork, continue ahead to reach a ladder stile by a metal gate followed by a junction a few metres further. Veer right there, following the 'Beentee Loop Walk' signpost, and walk up some steps to enter a small metal gate. Note: do not follow the Kerry Way signpost to the left.

You are now on the foothills of Carhan Upper. Daniel O'Connell, The

Liberator, was born in Carhan on 6 August 1775. The ruin of the house where he was born is near the twisting Carhan River in the broad valley to the north-east below. O'Connell, an important Irish political leader in the early nineteenth century, campaigned for Catholic Emancipation and the repeal of the Act of Union which combined Great Britain and Ireland.

Looking toward Knocknadobar from the Beentee ridge.

Follow a narrow path between fences to reach another small metal gate and ladder stile. Continue on a wide track to the left and reach another stile. The track then passes an enclosed field on the right which sometimes has livestock in it. Take a right when the path forks. Cross a ladder stile into a field with an abandoned house in an enclosed area adjacent to it. Reach another ladder stile with an electric fence to the left. Pass a farmhouse on the left then cross a further three ladder stiles before reaching a small metal gate with steps leading down and across a small stream.

This path leading to Gurteen was once an old Mass path during Penal times. A narrow path rises beyond the stream to meet a ladder stile. Cross the stile and follow the path as it passes a field on the left with a 'Beware of Bull' sign and an electric fence on its boundary. The narrow path then passes a small wooded area on the left with a ladder stile at its end. It crosses an open area soon after, before it is fringed by gorse and heather by an enclosed field on the right.

Cross further stiles to reach a tarmac road by a metal gate. Turn right at the road and pass a farm shed on the left. Look out for a ladder stile by a rusted metal gate on the right soon after at **V 494**47 **773**64, just before a patch of tall conifers. Follow the broad, stony track uphill keeping the conifers to the left. The track later veers right and away from the conifers. A few hundred metres further at **V 491**54 **774**46, leave the track and turn left to follow signposts uphill. A path runs to the right of a ditch and a stone wall covered with bracken and grass to arrive at the ridge top. Views north toward the Knocknadobar massif improve as height is gained.

Turn right at the ridge top, following a fence on the left initially. Cross three ladder stiles to arrive at a grassy col. From there, the path initially follows a fence then later veers left and away from it. The path leads gradually uphill, crossing two more ladder stiles, before reaching the broad grassy top of Beentee (*Binn an Tí*, 'peak of the house') which is marked by a

Cahersiveen, Valentia River, Foughil Island and Doulus Head from the summit of Beentee.

small pile of rocks by a fence at **V 476**10 **780**58.

The views from the summit are superb and extend as far as the Dingle Peninsula. To the west, a magnificent panorama sweeps northward from Valentia Island to Knocknadobar. Houses and buildings stretch across the banks of the Valentia River at Cahersiveen, a concrete strip amongst the network of fields that dominate its green plains. Further east, the collection of hills at Coomasaharn watch over the wide, green and brown plains, and Knocknadobar again dominates the landscape.

From the summit, descend the spur for around 150m, following a fence to the right and with Cahersiveen town also below on your right. Cross a ladder stile and continue a short distance to **V 474**79 **779**80 where there are two ladder stiles, one ahead and another to the right. Here, cross the stile on the right, following signs for 'Beentee Loop'.

Follow the path downhill, crossing another ladder stile before meeting a broad, eroded track. When the track bends left at **V 475**39 **784**09, leave it to continue straight downhill along the spur on a narrow grassy path. There are some conifers to the right. Note there is a signpost further down the path but not at the bend, so the path is easy to miss.

A few hundred metres downhill, the path veers left and away from the spur. As you descend, Cahersiveen should be to your right and the ground rising to your left. Feral goats and wild horses are commonly seen on the hillside here. After crossing a ladder stile, the path veers right and descends gently downhill passing some low gorse bushes to meet a ladder stile by a rusted metal gate at **V 469**27 **782**83.

Reach a small stream and cross two ladder stiles there then veer right immediately after. Cross three more ladder stiles before reaching the road, with the last stile located under a tree to the right of a metal gate.

Turn right on the road which is flanked by tall fuchsia bushes. After passing some houses the road runs above a standing stone in an enclosed field to the left at **V 467**62 **789**44. This ancient stone is about 2.5m (8ft) high and is named after the road, *Barr na Sráide* ('top of the street'), that runs above Cahersiveen.

Reach a junction on the left and continue ahead there along The Old Road. The Daniel O'Connell Memorial Church, the only Catholic church in Ireland named after a lay person, can be seen further to your left as you walk along the road passing some painted houses back to the start.

Knocknadobar From Roads

This is a complete traverse across the three summits of Iveragh North-West's most distinctive massifs.

Grade:	3
Distance:	11km (6¾ miles)
Ascent:	750m (2,461ft)
Time:	4–5 hours
Map:	OSi 1:50,000 Sheet 83

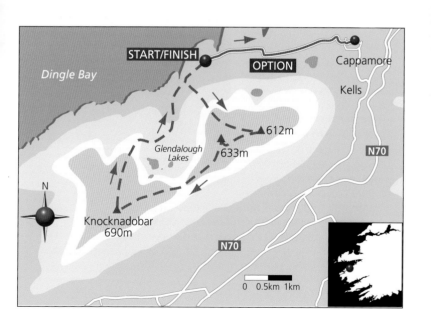

Start/Finish: Park at a lay-by of a lane where there is a single car space at **V 524**₉₉**874**₆₄, about 3.2km/2miles away from Kells Beach. There is alternative parking at Kells Beach itself at **V 556**₂₃ **878**₈₃, but this adds a distance of 6.4km/4miles and 1¾ to 2¼ hours to the total walking time.

Knocknadobar (690m/2,264ft) is a hill of pilgrimage. The Irish for Knocknadobar, *Cnoc na dTobar* means 'hill of the wells'. There is a large cross, called the Canon's Cross, just below its summit to the west. This cross is one of the stations that line its south-western slopes and was erected by Canon Brosnan, the parish priest of Cahersiveen in 1855. This route approaches the heights of Knocknadobar from the lonely townland of Roads, taking in two additional summits to the north-east of the massif – Kells Mountain (633m/2,077ft) and Kells Mountain East Top (612m/2,008ft) – along the way. Views of mountains and the sea from the top of the massif are stunning, and extend as far as the Dingle Peninsula.

Route Description

Walk south-westwards from the lay-by at the start point. Ignore the junction and continue straight ahead until meeting a metal gate. Go through the gate, and you will soon pass a cottage on the left. There are a further two metal gates. After the second metal gate at **V 520**₉₁ **870**₆₇, turn left and ascend the steep hillside above the townland of Roads in a south-easterly direction.

Looking down the south-west ridge of Knocknadobar with Valentia River, Cahersiveen and Beentee below.

The spur is grassy and coated with thick heather. Views behind across Dingle Bay and toward the Dingle Peninsula are good. Pass some stone-wall ruins midway up the slopes. These ruins are on a faint path that cuts diagonally across the slopes. It is traditionally known as *Cnoc na mBó* or 'hill of cows' as it was used once for herding cattle from Kells to Cahersiveen during traditional fairs.

Ignoring any diagonal paths, continue up the spur. It becomes stonier, with moss, short heather and some scattered rock later. A small cairn at point 568m at **V 527**₃₄ **862**₈₈ graces the top of the spur.

From here, head south-eastward to the col between Kells Mountain (summit 633m on the map) and Kells Mountain East Top (summit 612m on the map) on rough moorland. From the col, a slight rise eastward leads to a stony area of Kells Mountain East Top whose summit is marked by a cairn at **V 536**$_{33}$ **860**$_{31}$.

Descend back to the col, cross a broad gap, and then ascend the slopes leading to a large, stony area bounded by moss at Kells Mountain. There is a cairn at **V 528**$_{06}$ **858**$_{26}$.

From here, descend south-westward on a broad grassy ridge. The ridge is covered in white bog cotton, purple-pink ling heather and yellow tormentil in the summer. Just before reaching the broad col, there is a line of small upended stones at **V 523**$_{74}$ **852**$_{13}$ – a useful marker in the mist.

Walk across the col and then ascend the ridge leading west toward Knocknadobar. The ridge narrows in a section above the Glendalough Lakes nestling in a coum far below. You will eventually reach the shoulder where there is a large cairn of rocks at **V 511**$_{77}$ **846**$_{98}$. The summit of Knocknadobar is a distance of about 600m away from here on undulating ground south-west. A trig point and a ruined stone shelter marks the summit of Knocknadobar at **V 506**$_{49}$ **845**$_{16}$. The view from the summit is full of superlatives and includes nearly all of the mountains on the Iveragh and Dingle peninsulas.

It is now necessary to descend the spur leading north-eastward from the summit of Knocknadobar. The spur is stony and rocky at first, and then becomes steep and heather-clad. The Glendalough Lakes are huddled below in a rugged hollow and these come in view about 1.5km away from the summit of Knocknadobar at **V 511**$_{18}$ **858**$_{89}$. At this point, come off the spur, descending eastward down moderate slopes of grass and heather. There is a clump of large boulders about 300m away from the top of the spur at **V 513**$_{82}$ **858**$_{40}$. When you reach these boulders, veer north-eastward until hitting a stone-wall at **V 518**$_{12}$ **862**$_{45}$. A stream cuts through a small ravine to your right.

Head northward, keeping the stream to your right until you come to a path at **V 518**$_{07}$ **866**$_{41}$. Cross the stone bridge over the stream and follow the path north-eastward, which takes you back to the start point at the lay-by.

Looking eastward toward Kells Mountain and a panorama of Iveragh mountains from the summit of Knocknadobar.

37

ROUTE 6:
Knocknadobar via Stations of the Cross

Walk in the footsteps of ancient pilgrims and follow an airy crest to the top of an impressive mountain.

Grade:	3
Distance:	7km (4½ miles)
Ascent:	670m (2,198ft)
Time:	3–3½ hours
Map:	OSi 1:50,000 Sheet 83

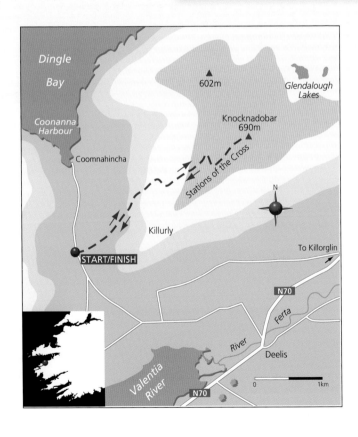

Start/finish: Drive across Cahersiveen bridge from the town and take a right around 800m (½ mile) after at crossroads. Continue on a narrow road marked as 'Ring of Kerry Cycle Route' on the OSi map for around 1.5km (1 mile) to reach a fork. Veer left at the fork and continue for another 1.25km (¾ mile) to reach a T-junction. Turn left there, pass a grotto on the right, and park at the lay-by on the left (space for a single car) just before an entrance to a farmhouse. There is another lay-by (also on the left) slightly beyond this entrance and under some trees at **V 480**$_{91}$ **829**$_{07}$, where there is space for a further two cars.

The Irish equivalent of Knocknadobar, *Cnoc na dTobar*, means 'hill of the wells'. In the book *Iveragh Peninsula: A Cultural Atlas of the Ring of Kerry*, Dr Tomás Ó Carragáin identifies Knocknadobar as a site of devotion to St Fursey (*c.* AD 597–650). Legend has it that the saint was cured of blindness at a holy well on the foothills of Killurly. An ancient pilgrim path leads up to the 690m (2,264ft) summit from the site of the holy well, now completely waymarked. Follow in the footsteps of medieval pilgrims who, on the last Sunday in July, would pray, dance and sing their way to the top.

Route Description

Cross the road and walk to a metal gate with a signpost 'Cnoc na dTobar'. Go through this gate and aim for another metal gate by a field on the right. Do not enter this gate, but rather follow a narrow path to its left. Yellow paint on rock and a green arrow on a thin white post indicate the route ahead.

Signpost at the foot of the Stations of the Cross route for Knocknadobar west of Killurly.

Follow this narrow path keeping a fence to your right. A grassy and rocky knoll rises to the left. Continue on the path to reach a metal gate. Follow the path beyond the gate to pass a concrete cross on a rock slab under a tree on the right.

This is the first of fourteen Stations placed at regular intervals up the mountain, with the route to the summit signposted throughout. The path meanders uphill amongst bracken and heather covered slopes, turning stony and rocky later. There are uplifting views to the west of Castlequin and its foothills, Coonanna Harbour and Killelan Mountain, a sweeping panorama that improves as height is gained.

The pilgrim route initially zigzags to the left of Knocknadobar's south-west ridge before veering right to reach the top of its airy crest. This is

The final section on the south-west ridge of Knocknadobar. The Stations of the Cross route bypasses the most exposed section of ridge here to the left (signposted 'Easier Route').

where spirits soar. The green and brown plains, fed by the Ferta and Carhan rivers, unfold as a wide expanse to the south-east. A backdrop of hills completes the picture, extending westward to hug the waters of the Valentia River and Portmagee Channel. The view down along the narrow ridge becomes more impressive as you climb toward the summit, with the coastline and headland at Canglass and Doulus, as well as Valentia Island, in the background.

Turn left on reaching the ridge and continue steeply to reach a huge concrete cross with a stone altar at **V 504**₄₇ **843**₇₆. Note: An 'Easier Route' (signposted) veers to the left and away from the ridge halfway along, with a further few Stations along the way. You may opt to continue along the airy ridge top, following a narrow path which later intersects with the Stations route before meeting the huge concrete cross and stone altar, erected by the Cahersiveen priest Canon Brosnan in 1885.

The slope eases beyond the concrete cross and continues for a few hundred metres to reach a trig pillar and a stone shelter at **V 506**₅₂ **845**₁₈, denoting the summit of Knocknadobar, on a broad, mossy top full of scattered rock. The view from the summit is full of superlatives and includes nearly all of the mountains on the Iveragh and Dingle peninsulas.

It is also interesting to note that the other two sacred sites of Brandon Mountain and Skellig Michael, both within sight, form a perfect triangle with Knocknadobar – coincidence? From here, peak-baggers may also wish to include the North Top (602m/1,975ft) a kilometre away to the north-east.

Having enjoyed the views, you may feel inclined to sing and dance, like the ancient pilgrims, down from the summit, by retracing steps back to the start.

Looking south-west from the large pilgrimage cross near the summit of Knocknadobar.

Variation: It is possible to link up Route 5 with this route if you have access to a second car. Follow directions as per Route 5 over Kells Mountain East Top (612m), Kells Mountain (633m) and to Knocknadobar. Instead of descending northward on the spur above Glendalough Lakes, come off the south-west ridge of Knocknadobar, then follow the Stations signposts off the mountain – essentially doing this route in reverse from the summit.

Lough Currane Circuit

A long, scenic circuit around one of the largest lakes on the western fringes of the Iveragh Peninsula.

Grade:	2/3 due to its length
Distance:	26km (16 miles)
Ascent:	400m (1,312ft)
Time:	7¼–9¼ hours
Map:	OSi 1:50,000 Sheet 83

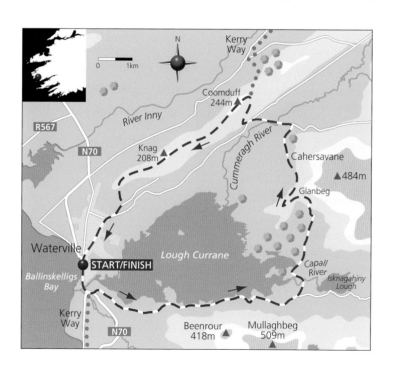

Start/finish: At the seafront in Waterville town. There are spaces to park along the main street near the Waterville Way Kerry Hostel at **V 503**₁₂ **659**₅₀, opposite the Charlie Chaplin statue. Save around 8km (5 miles) of road-walking at the start by getting a lift or taxi to the eastern end of Lough Currane at the junction where the Kerry Way veers north (O'Grady's Cabs, www.ogradyswaterville.com).

Waterville is sited on a narrow isthmus, with Lough Currane on the east and Ballinskelligs Bay on the west, and the Currane River linking the two. The 18th-century Butler family built an estate at the mouth of the river and named it Waterville. Traditionally, Waterville is known as *An Coireán*, meaning 'the crescent', descriptive of the bay that encircles it. Lough Currane stretches for nearly 6km (3¾ miles) to the east of the town. The lake was originally called Lough Lee and was said to have been formed after a deluge called up by the druids of the mythical Tuatha Dé Danann in their efforts to annihilate the marauding Milesians around 1600 BC. This route traces a section of the Kerry Way, one of Ireland's most popular walking trails, for nearly two-thirds of its length. It forms an easy but long circuit around Lough Currane, with fabulous views along a low-lying ridge at the end.

A steep section of the Kerry Way near Glanbeg, where care is needed during the descent.

Route Description

From the town, follow the N70 along the seafront for a few hundred metres. The N70 passes Waterville House on the right before crossing a bridge over River Currane. It passes Skellig Golf Club on the right before a bend. Turn left into a narrow road just after the bend, signposted 'Glenmore L7539'.

After passing the Waterville Lake Hotel on the left, the road meanders under the cover of trees for a length before winding above the southern fringes of Lough Currane. There are good views across the lake along some sections. After just over 7km of tarmac-bashing from Waterville Lake Hotel, reach a junction on the left at **V 566**₃₁ **650**₇₁.

Take a left along the byroad, which reduces to a track along some sections. Continue for around 3km, following Kerry Way signposts. Lough Currane is screened from view by trees on the left. Cross a bridge over the Capall River and pass some quarry workings before arriving at a junction with metal gates at **V 571**₀₃ **673**₇₆.

Veer left here and follow the lane uphill. The lane is flanked by enclosed fields backed by rugged hillside. At a fork around 200m away, veer right by a ruined building and pass under electric lines to reach a gate with a Walking Man symbol on it. Go uphill for around 100m and leave the track before a bend at **V 569**₃₃ **676**₇₄. Veer left there along a narrow path to reach a gate with a ladder stile and a Yellow Man signpost.

Stile and signposts below the summit of Coomduff, with Beenduff in the background. Our route veers left here toward Coomduff.

The path beyond the stile is fringed with fuchsia, foxgloves, tormentil and bracken. Around 100m further on, veer right uphill and cross a stream by a rhododendron bush. There is an abandoned house by a copse of trees on the slopes above. The Kerry Way then zigzags uphill, initially following a fence on the right, then passing an outcrop of boulders before swinging by a copse of trees. Pass a strip of gorse above on the right before veering right to reach a grassy shoulder near point 179m at Glanbeg, where there are expansive views of the valleys on either side of the spur.

The path descends slightly and contours along the hillside, following a fence on the left, toward Cahersavane. Cross a ladder stile by a rusted metal gate, go through an opening in the stone wall and follow signposts to reach a steep rocky section at **V 566**₆₂ **682**₅₆. Take care during the descent over this short stretch, particularly when the rocks are wet. All difficulties end upon reaching the valley floor below.

The Kerry Way is now flanked by knee-high bracken and soon reaches a surfaced lane by a house on the left. Lough Currane can be seen through a gap ahead. Turn right on the lane, pass an abandoned house and reach a metal gate with a ladder stile at a T-junction.

Turn right there and continue ahead to reach a bend in the road, with a ruined building ahead. Pass an enclosed field overgrown with – depending on the time of year – bracken, daffodils, foxgloves and tussocky grass immediately after the bend. The road is fringed by bracken, tall fuchsia trees, enclosed fields and a spruce forest.

It passes a metal gate at **V 562**₇₃ **697**₀₉ where there may still be a signpost labelled 'Kerry Way – Cahersiveen'. However, the Kerry Way has since been rerouted, as marked in the fourth edition of the OSi 1:50,000 Sheet 83 map. So continue along the road, passing a house by the patch of forestry ahead. Ignore a forest junction on the right and reach a T-junction around 300m further.

An Bheann Mhór and Coomcallee rising to the left of Lough Currane from Coomduff.

Turn left at the T-junction and follow the road over the Cummeragh River for another 1.2km or so to reach another junction. Turn left there and almost immediately take a right at a Y-junction soon after. Continue along the lane for around 150m before veering right to meet a grassy path leading uphill.

The path zigzags uphill to reach a ladder stile. On reaching a field, veer left to cross another stile then turn right to follow a fence and stone wall on the right. The path continues gradually uphill crossing two more stiles before reaching the top of a low-lying ridge. There is a ladder stile there, but do not cross it. Take a left (signposted Waterville), keep the fence to your right and traverse the ridge. There are ladder stiles in place throughout the ridge for the next 4.5km or so.

The first top on the ridge is Coomduff and is marked by a signpost. Here, expansive views unfold: the plains of the River Inny and Beenduff to the north; Lough Currane, Coomcallee and its backdrop of hills to the south; Ballinskelligs Bay and the Iveragh coastline to the west.

From Coomduff, a fence leads to a dip, followed by a gradual rise to Knag. The ground then undulates before veering left to descend off the ridge. A path follows a fence initially before reaching a stone enclosure with two metal gates and a stile. Go through this and several more metal gates to reach a house by a narrow road.

Take a right on the road towards Waterville. At the crossroads, turn right following signs for Waterville. Ignore the next junction on the right and continue downhill for just over 1km to reach a junction with a Londis shop ahead.

Turn left at the junction to meet the N70 and arrive back at the hostel.

Eagles Hill and Mullaghbeg

An enjoyable circuit above the scenic Lough Currane providing fabulous views of the area.

Grade:	3
Distance:	13km (8miles)
Ascent:	600m (1,968ft)
Time:	4¼–5¼ hours
Map:	OSi 1:50,000 Sheet 83

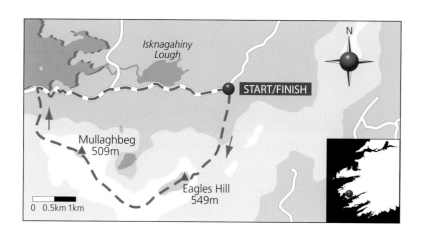

Start/Finish: Take the road east from Waterville after the Currane River, passing a hotel, and along a lane shaded by chestnut and sycamore trees. It winds along the long southern shores of Lough Currane. There are spaces for several cars at **V 593**₂₃ **651**₁₇ on the left of the road, just over a kilometre east of Isknagahiny Lough.

The landscape east of Waterville on the end of the Iveragh Peninsula is a fascinating combination of rugged ochre mountains, delightful blue lakes and verdant green valleys. There is a romantic charm about the place in these redeeming colours of nature. Routes 7, 8 and 9 suggest three routes for the hillwalker wishing to explore this area. The summits of Eagles Hill (549m/1,801ft) and Mullaghbeg (509m/1,670ft) are visited in this walk, but one of the main attractions are stunning high-level views of Lough Currane, a lake nearly 6km (3¾ miles) long.

Looking south-westwards towars the streaked peak of Eagles Hill from the slopes above Tooreenyduneen.

Route Description

Opposite the parking area, there is a Yellow Man sign, a 'Transforming Ireland' sign and a metal ladder stile. Go over the stile. A stony track leads to another metal ladder stile. Cross this, ignore the perpendicular track and continue uphill on a faint path under the cover of trees. The path is mossy and stony – look out for yellow arrows on the trunk of a tree a short distance away from the stile that confirms you are heading in the right direction.

Continue on the grassy path following the yellow arrows, until reaching a ladder stile at **V 593**₉₄ **649**₄₇ at the end of a green field. Now follow yellow markers, as the path passes a stone wall, and eventually brings you to a wooden stile where views of Eagles Hill start to unfold ahead.

You will soon arrive at a stream, cross it and continue to follow Yellow Man signs. The path, still grassy, is laden with bracken on both sides. A yellow arrow on a rock at **V 592**88 **643**35 points the required direction of travel. You will soon come to another stream, as the path weaves its way along some boulders and leads to a grassy area.

After a distance of about 500m uphill, you will reach a final stream. Cross this, and continue to follow Yellow Man signposts to the col between Windy Gap and Eagles Hill at **V 586**67 **632**21. As you ascend to the col passing under the rugged hillside on your left, notice the sheer ribs of sandstone rock tumbling down the northern spur of Eagles Hill to your right.

The col is a good place to rest before tackling Eagles Hill. For the keen, an optional hike up to a prominent knoll just east of the col provides good views of the steep profile of Eagles Hill towering above.

From the col, ascend the obvious grassy ramp to the right of a rock rib. There is also a line of fences tumbling down farther to the right. The going is steep, but mainly on grass. There is a broken section of fence at **V 585**51 **631**83. Ascend southward now on a moderately steep grassy slope for a distance of about 100m to reach a spur. Once on the spur, veer west toward the summit of Eagles Hill at **V 583**18 **630**91, marked by a single quartz rock. The eastern slopes of Mullaghbeg form a proud sweep out to the west, with Coomrooanig Lough below and the massive Lough Currane looming behind its broad dome.

From the summit, follow a fence leading south-westward, keeping it to the right until it turns a corner about 650m away at **V 577**72 **627**54. Continue descending south-westward, toward another fence that starts at **V 573**85 **624**67. Keep this fence to your left as you descend toward a peaty col. Once at the col, veer north-westward, over a gradual rise, then drop to a fence corner at **V 562**89 **630**81 where a broad track extends to the left. Do not take this track, but continue on north-westward ascending the gradual peaty ground to the 'soft' cairnless summit of Mullaghbeg at **V 559**25 **636**31, where the ground is firmer with grass and short heather.

It is best to walk to the northern rim of the plateau from the summit of Mullaghbeg for a panorama of Lough Currane and Isknagahiny Lough below, and the scratched sandstone slopes of Coomcallee to the north-east. The expansive water-sheet of reed-fringed Lough Currane is one of the most popular sea trout and spring salmon fisheries in Ireland, and is popular with anglers during its season. The sheltered waters of Ballinskelligs Bay, full of migrant sea birds, such as the common eider, common scoter and surf scoters throughout the winter, can also be seen westward.

Having savoured these wonderful views, descend west-north-west along a broad spur toward another peaty col. About a distance of 200m downhill, you will reach some fences at **V 557**43 **637**42; keep these to your left. Continue to descend the spur until arriving at a fence corner at **V 549**05 **640**69 just below the col. Cross this fence and descend the trackless ground of thick heather, keeping the stream to your right.

Midway down the mainly grassy slope at **V 550**30 **645**79 it relents and there are clumps of boulders. Aim for the following grid location on the descent: **V 549**10 **650**29 – it is roughly north of the previous grid location; and from above, a little promontory can be seen jutting out toward the lake near its location. On arrival, there is a concrete pillar at a fence by a rocky outcrop. Cross the fence, and carefully descend a rough patch of bare rock to reach the road.

A walk eastward of about 5km on the road leads back to the start point.

The view north from Mullaghbeg, with the easten end of Lough Currane below.

Coomcallee Circuit

A fabulous circuit above
an impressive glacial corrie
providing an intoxicating mix
of mountains, lakes, valleys
and the sea.

Grade:	3
Distance:	12.5km (7¾ miles)
Ascent:	720m (2,362ft)
Time:	4¼–5¼ hours
Map:	OSi 1:50,000 Sheet 83

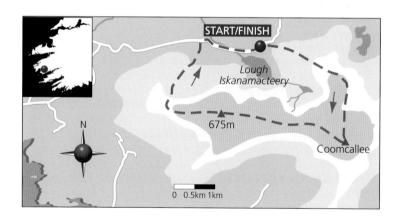

Start/Finish: Park at waste ground at **V 601**17 **698**35 or by a stone wall at a bend in the lane at **V 602**34 **699**04 east of the townland of Garreiny. This is best approached using minor roads leading eastwards from Waterville.

I f variety is the spice of life, then this is the walk for you: from lake-filled coums northward to wild scenery above an isolated valley to the east. Two peaks, Coomcallee (650m/2,133ft) and its West Top (675m/2,215ft) are taken in, followed by a descent on a narrow but easy ridge that provides fine views of Lough Currane and Ballinskelligs Bay.

Route Description

From the bend, walk eastward along the lane for a distance of about 100m. There is a metal gate on the right leading into a field. Go through this gate, and keeping fences to your right, walk uphill for another 100m to a second metal gate at **V 604**52 **699**57. A grassy path with scattered boulders goes steadily uphill by a stone walled fence on the right. After a distance of about 800m, the fence intersects, and slightly to its left is a step-stile at **V 612**32 **696**89. Cross this and continue south-eastward up the spur.

The fence soon turns right at a corner, and as you continue to gain height up the heather-clad spur, the surrounding view improves dramatically. It is one of striking beauty: behind you sits Lough Iskanamacteery ('lake of the esk') with its steep cliffs and gully above; to the north-north-west is the larger Cloonaghlin Lough and smaller Lough Namona along with an enchanting array of rolling Iveragh hills in the distant.

Continue uphill on this delightful stretch to **V 619**54 **693**43 where there is an area of small rock slabs. The spur starts to bend uphill to the right. At this stage, leave the spur and contour along east-south-eastward, keeping the higher ground on your right, and the chasmic plunge into the rugged glen dominated by Lough Coomeathcun below on your left. Ascend to a flat grassy area at **V 624**24 **691**06. Pause for a moment here, to appreciate the views toward the rugged ground around Lough Coomcurrane eastward: contorted Old Red Sandstone slabs, scratched as if by witches' claws, ripple like giant waves on the slopes of nameless peaks. Perhaps this is why the area is named after witches or hags, as Coomcallee or *Com Caillí* means 'corrie/hollow of the hag'.

From here, contour southwards for a distance of about 300m before descending to the grassy valley below. There are the remains of small ring forts at **V 623**23 **685**53 and continuing southward you will approach a stream on the left. Cross the stream where it forks and, maintaining southward progress, continue on uphill for a distance of about 100m to **V 623**56 **683**47. This is a lovely area: the stream with its small cascades and

Ascending the Maghygreenana spur with Lough Iskanamacteery and Coomcallee West Top behind.

rock pools, the valley with its ambience and remote setting. It makes an ideal lunch spot or a camping site.

After a well-deserved break, keep the stream to the left and ascend the grassy/mossy slope, passing a small waterfall along the way. The terrain now becomes increasingly stony/peaty nearer the summit of Coomcallee, which is at a fence intersection at **V 623**₉₅ **677**₃₁. The view southward across the Kenmare River and the Beara Peninsula beyond is striking, and so are the peaks of the Iveragh Peninsula to the east.

From the summit, head north-westward on a broad and grassy ridge. Follow a fence, keeping it on the left, to summit 642m. From here, swing westward as the ridge narrows. Just before a col, stop to gaze down the steep corrie to your right, where rocky spurs sweep down to its dark depths, and the edge of Lough Nambrackdarrig ('lake of the red trout') poking out behind some crags to your right.

Pass the col and ascend the slope westward. There is a horseshoe-shaped stone shelter just above the col at **V 606**₅₈ **681**₇₉. Follow a fence for most of the way up the slope to a stony, peaty plateau where you will meet another fence. Follow this, as the ground drops slightly again to another col. As you near the col, peep down the menacing gully north-eastward – full of rocky crags and a stream that flows down it to Lough Iskanamacteery further below. The gully is locally known as *Eisc na Mac tíre*, the 'steep path of the wolf'. Cloonaghlin Lough and Lough Namona lie in the distant, with the western tip of Derriana Lough further still.

Keep fences to your left and walk on mossy ground to its intersection at **V 595**₁₇ **683**₀₇ where there is a step-stile. Slightly higher, there is another

Lough Currane and Ballinskelligs Bay seen from the narrowest section of the ridge leading west from Coomcallee

step-stile leading to a trig point (on the opposite side of the fence) marking the summit of the West Top of Coomcallee at 675m/2,215ft.

Leaving the summit, cross the step-stile again and descend the ridge westward. At a distance of about 200m lower, the fence intersects, then later turns left at a corner. The heather-clad ridge narrows as you descend, passing some sharp upended rocks. This is a delightful stretch: there are steep drops on both sides of the ridge and fine lingering views, best at sunset, of Lough Currane and Ballinskelligs Bay in the distance.

A fence soon appears to the left: cross it at **V 583**30 **683**71, avoiding the obvious steeper ground to your left. However, you still have to pick your way down carefully amongst outcrops of boulders and heather to arrive at a fence corner at **V 581**48 **684**26. Cross this fence, and descend to the col east of Summit 484m.

At the col, descend north-east through trackless slopes of thick heather for a distance of about 300m until meeting a stony path at **V 581**82 **686**87. Follow this path downhill until you reach a metal gate. Go through this gate and continue on the track until around **V 586**71 **694**49, leaving it as it nears the leftmost tributary of a stream. Cross this and walk between two streams to a metal gate further below at **V 588**61 **696**32. Beyond this gate, there is a gap through the fence on the left. A green path between two fences conveniently leads you down to the road at **V 588**44 **700**45.

Once on the road, turn right and walk back for over a kilometre to the start point at the waste ground or the bend in the lane, giving ample time to reflect on the delights of the day.

Rossbeigh Strand

Fall in love with the golden
sands of Rossbeigh and enjoy
panoramic views of mountain
and sea.

Grade:	2
Distance:	6km (3¾ miles)
Ascent:	20m (66ft)
Time:	1½–2 hours
Map:	OSi 1:50,000 Sheet 78

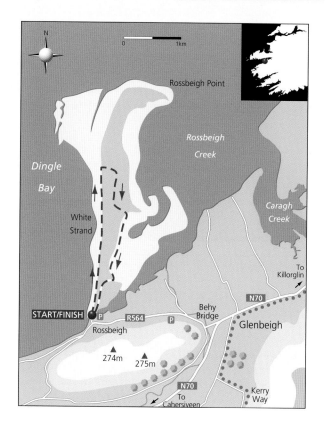

Start/finish: Leave the N70 at the end of Glenbeigh village, veering right on to the R564 to Rossbeigh. (Note: the OSi 1:50,000 4th edition map labels it 'Rossbehy'.) Continue for around 2.3km (1½ miles) along the R564 to reach a large car park on the right at Rossbeigh Strand at **V 645**11 **910**32. It is recommended to park as close to the entrance as possible so the full length of White Strand may be enjoyed.

Rossbeigh is a sandy peninsula to the west of Glenbeigh (*Gleann Beithe*, 'valley of the birch tree'), jutting for several kilometres into Dingle Bay. According to legend, it was here that the mythical figures of Oisin and Niamh galloped away on their white horse to the fabled island of Tir na nÓg ('land of youth'). Rossbeigh Strand becomes the venue for horse and pony racing in late August annually. The beach is also alive with sunbathers, swimmers and holidaymakers in the summer. This easy route wanders along the golden sands of White Strand and then crosses sand dunes to its opposite end at Rossbeigh Creek. Some easy navigation is needed to get across the dunes over a short stretch, giving the route a Grade 2 rating.

Looking across Dingle Bay on White Strand at Rossbeigh, with the mountains of the Dingle Peninsula in the distance.

Route Description

Drop down to the beach from the car park. Walk northward along the beautiful stretch of White Strand, sculpted by waves, with the dazzling blue waters of Dingle Bay to your left. Directly ahead across the bay is the Dingle Peninsula. Its mountains, which dance along the horizon, increase in size the farther along White Strand you go. A glance back to Rossbeigh reveals a line of hills too, characterised by the three humps of Curra Hill, a haunt for paragliders, and the conical profile of Drung Hill.

An abandoned boat at grassy sand dunes on the finger of land at Rossbeigh.

Farther along the strand, grassy sand dunes rise on the right. At the end of the dunes, there is a section of eroded beach, with the sea sweeping in at high tide. In 2008, over a thousand feet of Rossbeigh's sand dunes were swallowed by the sea. High tides, heavy rain and 130km/h gales at the turn of 2014 contributed toward further erosion.

The view ahead is good here, and the beach at Inch Strand visible across a channel of water, and the Slieve Mish mountains as a backdrop. If the tide is high, a channel of water will cut its way perpendicularly to the beach, barring the way ahead. It is important to note this as, when the tide is low, this channel of water may not be obvious.

Nevertheless, veer right and away from White Strand well before the end of the dunes. You will have walked around 2.5km along the beach from the car park at the start, provided you parked near the entrance. This amounts to around 40 to 50 minutes of continuous walking. There is no distinct feature here so the following GPS coordinates will help: **V 648**34 **935**69. Turn right there and follow an indistinct path along the grassy dunes for around 150m. The path goes up a slight rise and then across a flat, grassy area to reach an abandoned boat nearby at **V 649**65 **934**81.

Turn right at the boat and follow an informal and sandy path across a flat area through the dunes, with Curra Hill directly ahead in the distance. Pass a flat area of short grass surrounded by high tussocks around 300m further on. Continue straight ahead along the sandy path to reach another flat, grassy area another 300m further at **V 649**31 **929**28. Veer left here along a sandy path toward a grassy rise. Go up the slight rise and down again into a large, flat area overgrown with tussocky grass. Follow a narrow path through the tussocks for around 200m to reach a beach on the eastern end of Rossbeigh at **V 650**84 **927**69.

This beach is generally quieter than White Strand, although some cars take the liberty of driving along its sandy stretch at times, even though a signboard at the front prohibits it. Walk southward for just over a kilometre, with the sand and waters of Rossbeigh Creek to your left, to meet up with a broad track. This soon changes to a tarmac and leads back to the start.

Seefin Loop

This memorable route gives fine views over Castlemaine Harbour and Lough Caragh.

Grade:	3
Distance:	13.5km (8½ miles)
Ascent:	500m (1,640ft)
Time:	4¼–5¼ hours
Map:	OSi 1:50,000 Sheet 78

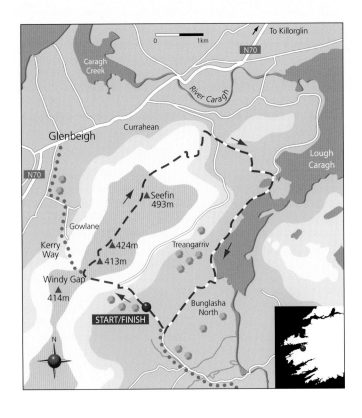

Start/finish: The start point is best approached from the N70. Take a left at a sharp bend approximately 8.5km (5¼ miles) after crossing Killorglin Bridge. Take a right at the next junction then drive along the western shores of Lough Caragh for several miles. Upon reaching the southern end of the lake, the road takes a sharp bend inland. Continue for just over 1.5km (1 mile), passing some houses and a sign for Glencar. Take a sharp right turn at the junction with Kerry Way signs just after a transmission mast. Drive along the boreen, passing a derelict school on the right. The boreen leads gradually uphill, with fine views of the hillside of Beenreagh to the left. After around 750m (½ mile), reach a small lay-by on the left at **V 688**₅₇ **876**₇₀. There are more spaces to park at a forest entrance a few metres ahead.

Lough Caragh, commonly referred to as Glencar Lake, is at the mouth of the fertile Glencar valley. It is a popular spot for recreational boat trips. The fish-shaped lake is noted for its spring salmon and grilse fishing, and to a lesser extent, for its brown trout and sea trout fishery. The hill of Seefin separates it from Glenbeigh to the west, its summit rising to 493m (1,617ft). This route follows the Kerry Way to Windy Gap, and then traverses the ridge to Seefin. A scenic stroll above the shoreline of the lovely Lough Caragh rounds off this memorable route.

The view north-east along Lough Caragh from the minor road at the foothills of Cosha North.

Route Description

Follow the boreen uphill. It soon turns into a gravel track and passes a green road by some trees on the left. Ignore this and continue uphill, passing an abandoned house at a bend in the track. Continue to a junction with a wooden bench on the right. Turn left here and head uphill on a grassy track toward a metal gate. Go through the gate and follow the track uphill towards the pass of Windy Gap. This section gives a foretaste of the scenery with sweeping views of the Corrawoolia and Coomavoon valleys, and the stretch of hillside from Beenreagh and Macklaun to the south. The track becomes stony and rocky as height is gained, before reaching a metal gate at the top of the pass.

Turn right at Windy Gap and go uphill along a stony path, keeping a fence on the right. Pass a large boulder and a small pile of rock. Leave the fence and veer left as the slope starts to relent. Aim for a grassy knoll with some exposed rock at **V 677**₂₇ **888**₆₇, around 200m north of point 413m.

57

Looking westward across Glenbeigh toward Curra Hill and Dingle Bay from the broad summit ridge of Seefin. Drung Hill and the Coomasaharn hills can be seen on the left.

Continue north-east on the broad, undulating and grassy ridge toward Seefin. Soon an informal path veers toward the fence again. Follow and cross the fence at a damaged stile, then continue uphill to reach a stony and rocky area with a standing stone at **V 683**₄₇ **893**₉₄. Lough Caragh now comes into sight, backed by green foothills that are dwarfed by the soaring peaks of the MacGillycuddy's Reeks beyond.

Cross an area of peat hags and heather along the broad ridge. A stiff pull up a stony slope leads to a small pile of rocks. Then the slope relents along a stony and rocky summit area to reach a trig pillar marking the summit of Seefin (*Suí Finn*, 'Fionn's seat') at **V 687**₈₈ **899**₅₉. Named after the mythical leader of the Fianna, Fionn mac Cumhaill, the summit provides fabulous views down to the shingle spit of Cromane (*An Cromán*, 'hip bone') and across Castlemaine Harbour to the Dingle Peninsula. Lough Caragh sits in a valley to the east, framed by a magnificent backdrop of the MacGillycuddy's Reeks to the right.

Descend north then north-west off the summit down a steep, stony slope. Aim for a track on a flat area below. During the descent, veer slightly left if the slope gets too steep. The slope becomes grassier and less steep along its lower sections. At any convenient point, dogleg to the right to meet intersecting tracks at **V 691**₀₉ **905**₀₅.

Continue straight ahead and along the wide stony track, with Seefin now rising to your right and Castlemaine Harbour below on your left. The northern end of Lough Caragh soon becomes visible along with the sharp hillocks rising above Callahaniska.

The view eastward from the summit of Seefin is dominated by the MacGillycuddy's Reeks.

Turn right on reaching a T-junction. The track passes the scattered debris of some rusted machinery before zigzagging further downhill to soon reach a metal gate by some trees within an enclosed area on the right. Lough Caragh and the MacGillycuddy's Reeks are constant features of the picturesque landscape ahead.

Go through the gate and follow the track downhill, ignoring an immediate junction on the right. Follow the track as it bends to the right and continue downhill to reach a crossroads. There is a large house with a gated compound and an upper viewing deck to the right just before the crossroads.

At the crossroads, take the branch leading downhill and south-east toward Lough Beg (this is the narrow road just left of the one signposted 'Kerry Way'). Pass some houses and farmhouses at a sharp bend before Lough Beg comes into view on the right.

Turn right at the T-junction and follow a narrow road which meanders along the western end of Lough Caragh. This is a delightful section, particularly as the road rises, revealing pretty views of Lough Caragh to the left. Later, the road dips into a valley and takes a sharp bend inland at the southern end of the lake.

Continue along the road for around 1.5km, passing some houses and a Glencar sign to arrive back at the Kerry Way junction just after the transmission mast. Turn right there and walk back to the start point.

The wide track marking the descent route from Seefin, with Lough Caragh and the MacGillycuddy's Reeks forming a picturesque backdrop.

ROUTE 12:

Coomasaharn Horseshoe

Visit wild, impressive, lake-filled and cliff-bound glacial coums in this gem of a walk.

Grade:	4
Distance:	14km (8¾ miles)
Ascent:	770m (2,526ft)
Time:	5–6 hours
Map:	OSi 1:50,000 Sheets 78 and 83

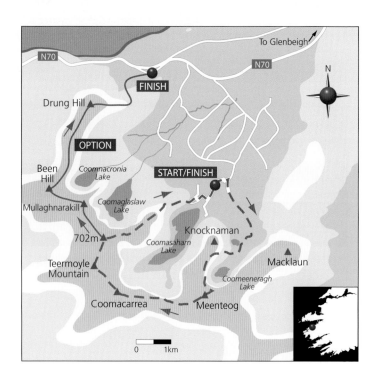

Start/finish: Take the minor road south-westward from Glenbeigh that leads into Coomasaharn. Near the lake, the road turns a sharp right. There is a track ahead with spaces for several cars on the side of the grassy verge around **V 636**28 **851**37. Alternative parking is also available on waste ground at **V 638**61 **855**45.

The ice ages have carved out six coums at the back of the sparsely populated valley south-west of Glenbeigh. The largest of these coums is Coomasaharn, which houses a lake about 2km long. This walk allows the hillwalker to peer down into Coomasaharn and four other coums in the area: some large and others small – but all untamed and rugged. It also takes in three summits, all above 600m/2,000ft: Meenteog (715m/2,346ft), Coomacarrea (772m/2,533ft) and Teermoyle Mountain (760m/2,493ft).

Route Description

Walk north-eastward away from the lake along the minor road, crossing a concrete bridge over the River Behy. About 250m away from the bridge at **V 642**32 **857**01 turn right, crossing a fence to meet a grassy track bordered by stone-wall fences. Walk for about 350m down this track until meeting a metal gate. Do not go through this gate but rather turn left uphill on a grassy and mossy slope.

Ascending the grassy and rocky spur south of Coomnagrossaun Lake with the broad ridge connecting Beenreagh and Seefin in the background.

Ascend the gradual slope in a south-easterly direction, admiring the views of the Knocknaman cliffs on your right. About a kilometre away, there is an area of boulders as you approach a stream on your right.

Cross this stream at **V 648**76 **844**22 and enter an area full of little streams running down the hillside, especially after a wet day. Ascend its boulder-strewn slopes, crossing further streams where necessary, but keeping the general down-flow to your right. There is a stone wall by some outcrops of boulders at **V 646**91 **840**10. Here, you are just below Coomnagrossaun Lake, and the next objective is to ascend the obvious rugged spur south of the lake leading up to Knocknaman's heights. There is a fine, sheltered spot at the bottom of this spur at **V 645**60 **837**40 by some sandstone rock slabs near a stream.

Ascend westward up the grassy and rocky spur. As you gain height, the lake below comes into sight, as well as the rugged slopes south toward Meenteog, and the gentler hillside of Macklaun (607m/1,991ft), Beenreagh (495m/1,624ft) and Seefin (493m/1,617ft) to the east/north-east. During my visit here, I saw a pair of mountain hares scampering up the spur, which becomes grassier as height is gained.

You will eventually reach the top of the spur just south of the summit of Knocknaman (561m/1,841ft), the 'hill of women'. Here, veer southwards to ascend the peaty and stony slopes towards Meenteog. Keep along its rim, as views of Coomeeneragh Lake and its rocky eastern cliffs appear menacingly below.

The terrain becomes grassier as you near a fence at **V 635**74 **827**88, and from here veer south-eastward to gain the summit of Meenteog: a boggy, flat and grassy patch, opposite a fence with no cairn at **V 638**03 **826**64. For a flat summit area, the encircling panoramic views of Dingle, the MacGillycuddy's Reeks, the Iveragh peaks and even the Skelligs more than compensate.

Descend south-westward from Meenteog to meet a fence at **V 630**99 **822**67, and follow this to reach a rusted metal gate. Go through this and as you near the col, there is another metal gate at **V 625**11 **823**81. There are remnants of an old boundary wall, but at the col, veer northward to descend slightly and peer over the edge – straight down into the hanging valley of Coomacullen in the abyss below. Coomacullen comes from the Irish *Cum a' Chuilinn*, meaning 'coum of the rolling incline': but from these heights it is more of a 'hollow of the plunging decline'! A tiny lake sits in its dark depths surrounded by vertiginous cliffs, and a waterway connects it to the larger Coomasaharn Lake below.

Rejoin the col, keep fences to your right and ascend a grassy spur to the summit of Coomacarrea, which is marked by small pile of rocks at **V 611**36 **825**24. Coomacarrea, or *Com an Chaorach* meaning 'hollow of the sheep', is also known locally as *Sagart*, the Irish for 'priest'. This is interesting as the OSi map marks the sheer cliff on its northern side as Leam-a-Soggarth, which translates to 'leap of the priest'. The religious association is also marked by local tradition of a Mass Rock deep in the coum during Penal times where worshippers would gather in secret, perhaps at dusk on a Saturday (*Satharn*). However, the name Coomasaharn more than likely dates back to ancient times before the Penal era.

From Coomacarrea's summit set a course north-west toward the broad col between it and Teermoyle Mountain. Its summit is on an equally broad plateau, so you may have to walk on a bearing to get to its top which is marked by a small pile of rocks on a lump of peat at **V 603**97 **832**91.

Descend north-eastward from Teermoyle Mountain over broad slopes of peat. There is a fence on a level grassy area at **V 606**20 **841**26, and the spur leading to Coomreagh appears in sight. This is the spur you must descend on.

Extended variation: From Teermoyle Mountain, it is possible to continue north-westward instead of dropping down the Ceimaconaire spur; taking in the summits of Mullaghnarakill (665m/2,182ft), Been Hill (651m/2,136ft), Beenmore (660m/2,165ft) and Drung Hill (640m/2,100ft), and passing above Coomaglaslaw and Coomnacronia en route. However, this ideally requires a second car parked to the west of Mountain Stage at around **V 620**₀₀ **887**₀₀. The descent route off Drung Hill is via its eastern spur, veering off north-westward around **V 614**₀₀ **878**₀₀ and then north-eastward to meet the Kerry Way. The total distance for this Grade 4 variation is 18km/11¼miles, a total ascent of 1,060m/3,478ft, 6¼ to 7¾ hours' walking time.

There are views of Coomaglaslaw Lake to the north as you descend, but your attention will probably be drawn to the steep grassy drop to the narrow arête, known locally as Ceimaconaire, ahead. This is easier than it looks, nevertheless care must be heeded over this relatively short section. The ridge is a delightful traverse and there are breathtaking views of Coomasaharn's amphitheatre below.

Looking down into Coomacullen from the col east of Coomacarrea, with Coomasaharn Lake behind, and the mountains of Dingle afar.

Coomasaharn is a place where I often see ravens soar in pairs, filling the skies with their resonant '*pruck*' call. At the end of the coum is an area in which locals believe that Ireland's last wolf was pursued and killed by hunters who travelled from as far as Mayo! The waters of Coomasaharn are also said to be inhabited by a unique Irish form of Arctic char, the *Salvelinus fimbriatus* (*fimbriatus* means 'fringed').

The terrain becomes comfortable again around **V 611**₆₆ **841**₈₅. Descend undulating grassy slopes, which later become moderately steep after just over a kilometre, to a fence at **V 623**₇₄ **850**₁₈. Here, swing eastward and descend somewhat steeply down the slope of short grass and boulders to reach a dirt track at **V 625**₅₂ **849**₉₇. Turn left down this track to reach a metal gate at **V 631**₃₅ **851**₀₇. Go through this gate, turning left. Here, look out for several rock surfaces decorated with circles, lines and rings: ancient rock art.

Continue on for a distance of about 200m, before turning right near some buildings on a stony track that leads you down to a tarmac road below. Turn left at the tarmac road and simply follow this back to the start point.

Coomaclarig and Curravaha Horseshoe

This is a tough walk over four rugged summits around a remote valley near Glencar.

Normal Route
Grade: 4
Distance: 13.5km (8½ miles)
Ascent: 900m (2,953ft)
Time 5–6 hours
Map: OSi 1:50,000 Sheet 78

Short variation
Grade: 3
Distance: 10km (6¼ miles)
Ascent: 640m (2,100ft)
Time 3½–4½ hours
Map: OSi 1:50,000 Sheet 78

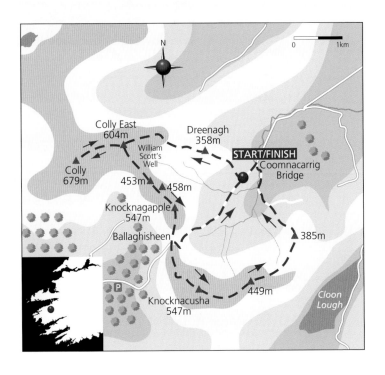

Start/finish: Coming from Killorglin, turn left along a minor road signposted Glencar at the top of the street after Killorglin Bridge. Continue for around 1.2km (¾ mile), then turn right and drive for another 7.2km (4½ miles) toward Glencar. Ignore all junctions and crossroads along that stretch to reach a T-junction. Turn right and continue for another 4km (2½ miles) to reach Lough Acoose. Drive past Lough Acoose on the left to reach a Y-junction. Take a left here and continue for another 3.5km (2¼ miles) to reach a T-junction. Turn right here at Bealalaw Bridge and drive over the River Caragh. The road narrows beyond that point and goes gradually uphill before levelling off along a wide valley. Continue for another 4.5km (2¾ miles), crossing Dromalonhurt Bridge, Kealboy Bridge and Coomnacarrig Bridge before arriving at a lay-by at **V 684**87 **803**80 where there are spaces for two cars.

This circular route explores some rugged hills on the southern fringes of the Glenbeigh Mountains and the northern end of the Dunkerron Mountains. The approach is via a wide, barren valley to the east of the range, accessible through a narrow mountain road from Glencar. It gives a good foretaste of the area before harder routes like Knockmoyle (Route 14) and The Cloon Horseshoe (Route 15) are attempted. The summits visited in this route are Colly East (604m/1,982ft), Colly (679m/2,228ft), Knockagapple (466m/1,529ft) and Knocknacusha (547m/1,795ft).

Route Description

Walk across moorland and ascend the slopes toward Dreenagh to the north-west. The ground can be boggy underfoot initially, especially after a wet day. The terrain is firmer on short grass after passing a stone wall and the ruins of a stone building. Ascend the moderately steep slope using grassy ramps to bypass rock slabs. Continue along the spur to reach Dreenagh, whose slopes are flanked by expansive valleys. The entire horseshoe of the route from Colly East to Knocknacusha can be studied from here.

The ground undulates before descending to a col. There is an erratic at **V 673**04 **810**21 which serves as a navigational aid in the mist. Ascend the moderately steep slope beyond the col. The ground is initially grassy and mossy with scattered rock and boulders, and then

The fence-line leading to Colly from Colly East.

Coomura and Knockmoyle from the summit of Knocknacusha.

becomes heathery nearer the top of the ridge. Turn left on the ridge and continue to Colly East, whose summit is marked by the corner of a fence at **V 660**$_{29}$ **810**$_{72}$.

Follow the fence from there to the pyramidal summit of Colly, about a kilometre away, and then retrace steps back to Colly East. This is a straightforward section with fabulous views down to the valleys on both sides of the ridge – the barren Cummernabarnadarriga Glen on the right and the more fertile Shronaloughane and Derreennageeha valleys to the left.

Back on Colly East, descend south-eastwards on a steep slope above the natural pool of William Scott's Well, reputedly named after a man who died at this spot, and from where a stream issues. A fence leads to the col below. Follow the fence to its corner at **V 665**$_{46}$ **804**$_{49}$ and cross it there. Keep to the right of the fence to avoid steep ground on the left.

Keep following the fence on undulating ground for around 850m to reach the base of a rocky crag at **V 670**$_{44}$ **798**$_{56}$. Veer left to bypass the crag and ascend a steep slope to reach the rocky and grassy top of Knocknagapple.

The aim now is to reach the top of the road at Ballaghisheen Pass. Some rough and steep ground needs to be negotiated along this section. Descend southward from Knocknagapple, following a fence initially, but later cross and veer away from it to avoid steep ground on the left. A wide, forested valley can be seen below on the right.

Reach a flat, rugged area then descend steeply, picking your way down rock benches via grassy ramps until reaching the road. Note: no difficult or committing scrambling moves should be required.

Short variation: If you have had enough upon reaching the road at Ballaghisheen Pass, then turn left and follow the road downhill for just over 2km to reach the lay-by at the start. Do not underestimate the terrain onward to Knocknacusha, point 449m and point 385m – it can be quite rough.

Cross the road and a fence to ascend southward, later veering south-eastward, on a rugged spur to reach the summit of Knocknacusha (*Cnoc Osaidh*, 'hill of the encampment'). This is an even better vantage point than Colly. From here, one is rewarded with a stunning panorama from the MacGillycuddy's Reeks to Broaghnabinnia, then across Knockaunanattin and down to the Ballaghbeama Gap, up again to Mullaghanattin then along the Beann ridge, and finally across primeval ground to Coomura and Knockmoyle.

It is difficult to leave Knocknacusha, but leave it we must. Keep to the spine of the spur and descend initially south-eastward then later veer east-north-east to reach a complex col before a slight rise to point 449m. At this point, the Curravaha valley spreads to the left and the waters of Cloon Lough shimmer below to the right. Keeping the Curravaha valley to the left, descend trackless and rugged ground by doglegging to point 385m, approximately 1.4km away.

Descend north-westwards from point 385m, aiming for a gate at **V 690**32 **798**38 at a track below. Go through the gate with care, turn left on the track and continue for around a kilometre to reach a T-junction.

Turn left again, cross Coomnacarrig Bridge, and walk back to the start.

Looking eastward toward a panorama of Iveragh mountains from the summit of Knocknacusha.

Coomnacronia, Knockmoyle and Knocknagantee

Explore the three rugged hills above Derrynagree and enjoy superb views of hidden corries and distant Iveragh peaks.

Grade:	3
Distance:	11km/6¾ miles from **V 675**₁₆ **706**₉₀
Ascent:	820m (2,690ft)
Time:	4–5 hours
Map:	OSi 1:50,000 Sheet 78

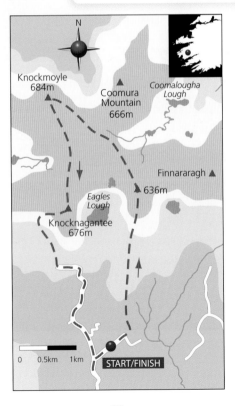

Start/finish: At **V 675**₁₆ **706**₉₀ on a minor road north-west of Sneem that follows the twisty course of its namesake river. There is a lay-by opposite a farm building. Park here with consideration and not to block any gates. If it is not possible to park opposite the farm building, there are spaces at a lay-by at **V 672**₉₈ **702**₅₂ for 3 to 4 cars. If parking here, then add a further 500m to the walk.

A river flows from the north-west in a knot-like fashion and swirls when it meets the currents of Kenmare River in an estuary south of a village. This is reminiscent of the place-name meaning of its village, Sneem (*An tSnaidhm*, 'the knot'). At the upper reaches of the Sneem River, its many tributaries gush down as delightful mountain streams from its rugged heights. This walk explores the high places north of the river, above the townland of Derrynagree, taking in three hills separated by a broad expanse of moorland but offering wonderful views of lower coums and distant peaks. These hills are Coomnacronia (636m/2,087ft), Knockmoyle (684m/2,244ft) and Knocknagantee (676m/2,218ft).

Eagles Lough and the sheer east face of Knocknagantee, as seen from Coomnacronia.

Route Description

Walk north-eastward uphill on the tarmac for about 300m until reaching a metal gate with a ladder stile at **V 677**₆₁ **708**₈₅, just beyond a bungalow on the left. Go over this stile. You will soon arrive at another metal gate also with a ladder stile. Beyond this stile is a large dwelling and beyond it is a metal gate with a smaller gate on its right. Pass a building on your left, and then arrive at yet another metal gate also with a smaller gate and a brown Fáilte Ireland and National Development Plan sign at **V 678**₉₇ **709**₉₄. Ascend left and northward up the grassy slopes beyond this gate, skirting between clumps of rock and gorse patches.

Cross a barbed-wire fence carefully after a distance of about 200m uphill. Beyond this and another 500m uphill, the fence intersects at **V 678**67 **716**36. Here, cross the fence that runs down the mountain, then walk 12 or more double paces following the barbed fence perpendicular to the slope, and cross it at a convenient point. Having surmounted this fence, you are now on the open mountain.

Ascend the moderate grassy slopes decorated with bell heather, bog cotton, butterwort and sphagnum moss. The inviting outline of Knocknagantee and Coomnacronia looms above as you ascent into the bosom of the mountain. The slope steepens when Eagles Lough comes into sight below on your left. It becomes littered with scattered rock and relents as you near the summit area. A small pile of rocks marks the summit of Coomnacronia (*Com na Cróine*, 'hollow of the red cow') at **V 679**92 **733**31.

For the best views, detour about 100m west of the summit to the edge of the plateau to stare directly down the impressive coum that holds Eagles Lough and the rocky terrain leading up to the higher valley of Coomanassig (*Com an Easaigh*, 'coum of the waterfall'), holding a smaller lake. On wet days, a spectacular waterfall sprays down from it into Eagles Lough below. You will also look directly across to the triangular profile of Knocknagantee, the last hill you will ascend in this walk.

There is a line of fences about 100m north of the summit. Follow these north-westward for another 300m before leaving it at **V 678**64 **736**76. Continue north-westwards, weaving along broad, grassy ledges between rock slabs and boulders before descending to a peaty and boggy col. If you care to look north-eastward during the descent, you will catch a glimpse of some lakes trapped on rock shelves, an area we will visit in the next walk.

Just beyond the col to the north-west, some fences intersect at **V 675**23 **742**74 as the ground starts to rise again. Cross the fence on your

Looking towards the slopes above Coomura from below the summit of Knockmoyle.

70

The rugged view westwards from the summit of Knocknagantee.

right, and keep the line of fences now to your left. The terrain is initially boulder strewn, then later boggy and grassy, as the fence intersects twice again before you reach the bald and rounded hill of Knockmoyle at **V 665**11 **749**80, marked by a pile of small rock slabs. There are good views down into Coomura to the east; the wide, barren valley of Maulnabrack below; and the southern corner of the Coomasaharn hills beyond.

Cross a fence near the summit and descend southward for about 300m to a peaty area at **V 665**73 **747**08. Here, start to veer south-eastward to reach close to a stream, which may not be apparent during dry periods, at **V 668**38 **742**15. From here, walk on a southward course, following a line of fences down a boggy and rocky gap, before it starts to rise again. Continue southward uphill, passing a ladder stile on your right, just before the beehive cairn that marks the summit of Knocknagantee at **V 667**97 **729**93.

Knocknagantee is one of the three triangulation points on the Iveragh Peninsula for the Ordnance Survey mapping activities of 1825 to 1833, and understandably so. A wonderful panorama of the surrounding peninsulas of Beara and Iveragh beckons. The views of the complex ground toward Coomcallee toward the west and the small jagged dots of the Skelligs out to sea are also good. It is a good place then to enjoy far-reaching views, a snack and a conversation. In days of yore, locals would claim that groups of people would meet here while out tending sheep. On both accounts, perhaps the summit is deserving of its name: *Cnoc na gCainnte* or 'hill of conversation'.

Walk back to the ladder stile, cross it, and descend roughly westward down grassy and rocky slopes to meet a distinct track at **V 663**10 **729**51. Follow this track to reach a metal gate at **V 670**63 **715**50. Then follow the road downhill as it passes by some farm buildings. After about a kilometre, turn left at the junction at **V 672**80 **70**500 if you parked opposite the initial farm building. If not, carry on along the road to the alternative start point.

ROUTE 15:

The Cloon Horseshoe

This challenging and committing mountain walk is probably the wildest and roughest in all of Ireland.

Grade:	5
Distance:	17km (10¾ miles)
Ascent:	1,200m (3,773ft)
Time:	7 to 8½ hours, time added for difficulty of terrain
Map:	OSi 1:50,000 Sheet 78

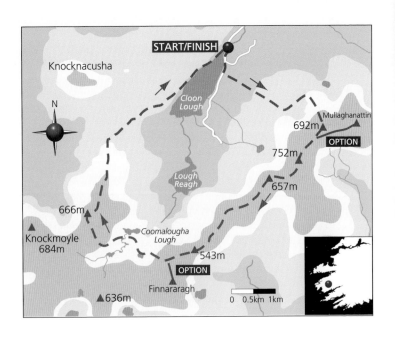

Start/finish: At the north-eastern end of Cloon Lough at **V 708**94 **788**91 just before the minor road crosses the Owenroe River. You may approach the start point via Beaufort–Lough Acoose from the north or via Moll's Gap–Gearha South–Ballaghbeama Gap from the south. The minor road along Ballaghbeama Gap is a narrow ribbon of road flanked by bare rock, especially at the top of the pass. Either way, allow plenty of time for the drive to the start point.

The mountains of Kerry are older than the Alps and even the Himalaya: hundreds of millions of years of geological evolution have been etched into their complex and contorted folds. This route, one of my favourite circuits in Ireland, bears testament to that. This horseshoe is best reserved for a clear day and should be undertaken by experienced hillwalkers only. In the winter, this walk can be a serious proposition.

Route Description

Cross the bridge over the river and walk along a boreen with Cloon Lough to your right. After a few hundred metres, pass a junction on the left which leads to a farmhouse. Continue straight ahead and after a further 200m, reach a stream at **V 708**41 **783**90. Leave the boreen and turn left to ascend a grassy, boggy slope in a south-east direction. Keep the stream to your left and soon pass under electric lines. A huge boulder at **V 713**49 **781**00 is a useful guide in the mist. The stream soon peters out after this boulder. Another stream, flowing through a narrow ravine, appears on the left further upslope. Continue to a flat area at **V 725**00 **774**00 adorned with cliffs forming a rocky amphitheatre at its far end. Cross the stream with care and veer north-east to ascend a gentle slope until reaching the top of a spur overlooking Eskabehy Lough below.

At this point, the spur veers southward. However, you might want to stop awhile to appreciate the views north-eastward of the MacGillycuddy's Reeks and a range of Iveragh peaks in the distant. Closer at hand, the northern spur of Mullaghanattin also features, rising sharply nearer its summit.

Looking north-east towards the MacGillycuddy's Reeks and Broaghnabinnia from slopes high above Eskabehy Lough.

73

Follow the spine of the spur steeply upward, outflanking a jumble of boulders at **V 729**44 **775**67 to its right, and at the first opportunity, ascend a grassy ramp to regain the spur. Keep a lookout for St Patrick's Cabbage trapped in rocky nooks and crannies as you zigzag up the grassy slope. A stiff pull between rocky outcrops brings you on point 692m, a subsidiary top of Beann, at **V 730**60 **770**98.

Mullaghanattin extension: From summit 692m, one mountain stands out above the rest. It displays a monstrous triangular form whose apex seems to touch the clouds. The mountain, Mullaghanattin (773m/2,536ft), is known as 'the Matterhorn of Kerry' due to this profile. An out-and-back to its lofty perch can be undertaken by descending steeply to the col due east of point 692m, and then ascending north-eastward up a steep grassy treadmill to its trig point. On the return, there is no need to climb back up to point 692m again: just follow the fence to reach the col south-west of it. Allow just over an hour for this extension.

Mullaghanattin as seen from summit 692m, a subsidiary top north-east of Beann.

Descend the grassy ridge south-west toward a small col. Next, ascend the slopes beyond, following a fence on the narrow grassy ridge to point 752m, a top known locally as Beann. Views along the ridge toward the south-west and down to the valley that holds Cloon Lough and Lough Reagh below on your right are good throughout the ridge walk.

Continue south-westward from here, crossing some fences along the way. After about 300m at **V 724**58 **761**58, you will reach a fence intersection and the spur branches into two directions. Here, head westward: cross the fence and handrail its line (keeping it to your right) with care, down a steep grassy slope toward a col.

Nestled lakes tucked between fangs of rock above precipitous headwalls at Coolyvrack, south of Lough Reagh.

The fence intersects at the col. Cross this and ascend another steep grassy slope to gain another subsidiary top of Beann: point 657m. The summit area is grassy with some rock slabs.

From here, head south-westward along the ridge. After about 400m at **V 716**$_{31}$ **756**$_{49}$, veer left to avoid a hazardous drop down a rocky crag. Pass under a rock rib on the left. Soon after, the ridge undulates on grassy and peaty terrain over point 636m and point 619m. It then drops down a grassy gap before rising again amidst some rocky outcrops to a summit area of 570m, flanked by huge slabs of rock.

Next, pick your way along rocky outcrops to point 543m at **V 701**$_{41}$ **744**$_{00}$. The following section – the descent into the area where the nestled lakes sit – is navigationally challenging: even on a clear day. To assist you at this point, walk on a bearing of 254º, making appropriate adjustments for magnetic variation, for a distance of 700m to **V 694**$_{25}$ **742**$_{45}$.

Initially, there are rocky slabs ahead and boulder-strewn ground to the right of it. Descend carefully from point 543m into a rugged area, following the bearing. The ground rises again soon after. Beyond this, you will be out of the boulder-strewn area. The ground now undulates and is a mix of rough grass and heather until you arrive near a stream at **V 694**$_{25}$ **742**$_{45}$. If you have crossed the stream you have gone too far.

Finnararagh extension: Near the stream at **V 694**$_{25}$ **742**$_{45}$, head south-eastward up rugged slopes for a distance of 500m, to reach the summit of Finnararagh (667m/ 2,188ft), marked by a small cairn. Allow about 30–40 minutes for this extension.

With the stream on your left, carefully pick a route down rock slabs and heather-clad ground. After descending a distance of about 400m, you will reach a stream junction at **V 690**$_{97}$ **744**$_{20}$ on a level grassy floor. Here, veer left and ascend south-westward up a slight rise to a lake. The scenery here gives a foretaste of things to come: the lake is tucked in a lonely niche, surrounded by forbidding cliffs. Descend to the northern corner of the lake, and cross the stream flowing away from it.

Keep this stream on your right and follow it northward. After a distance of around 200m, you will reach a rocky outcrop the size of a house on your left at **V 688**$_{30}$ **746**$_{07}$. Outflank this outcrop, and veer north-westward for about 150m, aiming for a large slab of rock slightly above, ahead at **V 687**$_{40}$ **747**$_{59}$. You are now above Coomalougha Lough, and it doesn't get any wilder than this throughout all the mountains of Kerry, perhaps all of Ireland. The wild landscape here is barren and austere: trapped lakes, rocky fangs, sandstone slabs and sheer cliffs – a primeval world!

Next, head westward, aiming for the southern end of the stream that feeds the larger lake below from the tiny upper one at **V 685**$_{86}$ **747**$_{25}$. Cross this with care, and perhaps notice the purple butterwort and forest-green fir club moss adding a touch of colour to the rocky surroundings in spring. Walk westward on a rock slab for about 100m until reaching a fence at **V 684**$_{86}$ **747**$_{57}$.

At present, rocky crags tower above. Ascend a grassy ramp south-westward with these crags above on your right. A chain of paternoster lakes lies below on your left. Continue for a distance of about 400m, until you are above the last lake in this chain at **V 681**$_{28}$ **745**$_{22}$, and the slope above is no longer rocky but grassy. Now face up the incline and ascend the moderate slopes to the grassy summit of Coomura Mountain (666m/2,185ft) at **V 677**$_{24}$ **751**$_{83}$. The view down to its coum is impressive, with the steep eastern slopes of Knockmoyle across, and the wide Coombaha valley below.

Descend the grassy spur leading north-eastward from Coomura Mountain. About 200m away from point 532m, at **V 681**$_{88}$ **761**$_{29}$ the ground becomes littered with rock slabs barring your descent.

It is now very rough going until you reach the rugged col below. Head northward, weaving your way between large rock outcrops, picking the least line of resistance (it is easier if you veer slightly to the left). Later, descend a grassy and rocky ramp between some rock slabs to **V 682**$_{57}$ **764**$_{88}$. Beyond this, descend steeply below a rock band above to your left to finally arrive at the complex col (elevation: 275m) just above the Glasheenoerreen Stream at **V 682**$_{26}$ **769**$_{06}$.

Notice two zinc-roofed buildings on your right: walk in the direction of the lower one, descending the moderately steep boggy ground that is littered with compact rush. Sounds of water gush down from a stream on your left. Cross the stream about 500m away at **V 686**$_{27}$ **772**$_{25}$ and reach a wall 100m beyond this at **V 686**$_{91}$ **773**$_{01}$ among some gorse bushes. Keep the wall to your left to eventually reach a fence corner about 150m away at **V 687**$_{97}$ **773**$_{56}$. Keep the fence to your left and follow the wall. Cross a fence soon after and continue to follow the wall, passing a ruined enclosure along the way to finally reach a muddy track at **V 689**$_{75}$ **774**$_{91}$.

The track improves upon reaching a metal gate soon after. At **V 691**$_{81}$ **776**$_{00}$, the track forks; take the right fork. The track now becomes stony, as you pass another gate and a sheep enclosure. It then bends right and meanders by the expansive waters of Cloon Lough.

There is a small crannóg on the lake and the entire mountain range you walked on earlier rises above Cloon Lough to your right, with the menacing cliffs above Lough Reagh in its furthest reaches.

The going is now easy: simply follow the fine track along the idyllic and expansive waters of Cloon Lough back to the start point on its north-eastern end, perhaps under darkening skies after a long but rewarding day.

Gearhameen Circuit

Visit a delightful waterfall and trace a fine high-level circuit around a remote valley with stunning views across to the MacGillycuddy's Reeks.

Grade:	4
Distance:	11km (6¾ miles)
Ascent:	830m (2,723ft)
Time:	4–5 hours
Map:	OSi 1:50,000 Sheet 78, OSi 1:25,000 Adventure Series *MacGillycuddy's Reeks & Killarney National Park* or Harvey Superwalker 1:30,000 *MacGillycuddy's Reeks & Killarney National Park*

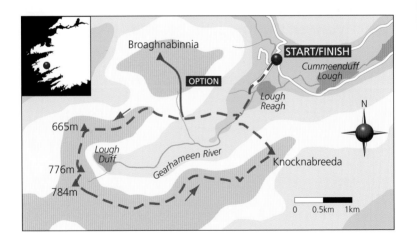

Start/Finish: Across a concrete bridge over the Cummeenduff River at **V 821**$_{78}$ **813**$_{01}$ where there are spaces for five to six cars on the left.

This is a walk with amazing variety. Getting to the start point may be an experience in itself, as it involves a long drive into the depths of the Black Valley and then into the remote Cummeenduff Glen beyond. The area around Lough Reagh is charming: with its lake, stream and waterfall. The rest of the walk is a circuit around the upper reaches of the Gearhameen valley, which is surrounded by a horseshoe of peaks ranging from Broaghnabinnia (745m/2,444ft), and Stumpa Duloigh (784m/2,572ft) and to Knocknabreeda (569m/1,876ft).

Route Description

The Black Valley, with its few dwellings, a church and a youth hostel on a single-track road, is a 'forgotten valley'. Electricity arrived only in 1977, justifying its name somewhat, and the first telephone in 1990. The Irish word, *duff* or *dubh*, for 'black', is associated with the river, lake, glens and mountain in the area: Black Valley, Cummeenduff River, Cummeenduff Glen, Lough Duff, Stumpa Duloigh.

Access to the Black Valley can be made either via a long winding road from Moll's Gap or a shorter narrow road through the Gap of Dunloe. South-west of it is Cummeenduff Glen, a picturesque valley with a distinctive alpine air.

From the parking space, cross the bridge over the Cummeenduff River and take a right turn down a lane just after it, going through two metal gates. The lane soon forks. Take the left fork and go through another two gates to reach a track. The track meanders around the edge of Lough Reagh, and during my last visit here there was a white swan swimming in the idyllic waters of the lake. A lovely waterfall can be seen tumbling down from higher ground above the lake.

Ascend the boulder-strewn ground leading up to the waterfall by zigzagging along a grassy ramp among some rocky outcrops. This is an area of tumbling boulders, gurgling rock-pools, delightful cascades and where black feral goats roam amongst the green bracken.

Aim for a grassy ledge at **V 815**$_{56}$ **804**$_{37}$, a perfect place to admire the plunge of the waterfall at close quarters. The area is like a 'little garden of Eden' in the spring and summer: St Patrick's Cabbage grows in rock crevices; purple butterwort graces the lichen rock; yellow primroses, purple dog-violets, bog pimpernel and yellow lesser celandine decorate the ground. There are also fabulous views of Lough Reagh, Cummeenduff Glen and Brassel Mountain to the north-east, making it difficult to leave this heavenly place.

But leave you must, and head for the upper valley above. Here you will enteralmostanotherworld,sodifferentisitfromthevalleybelow.Itiscommon to see ravens soaring in the skies above. The view by some large rock slabs at **V 814**34 **804**24 down to the three lakes in Cummeenduff Glen is particularly good. At this point, ascend the grassy and rocky ground on a spur leading westward above the Gearhameen River. After a distance of around 350m, the ground is littered with boulders and there are some stone circles at **V 810**68 **804**48.

The entire route ahead now opens up: a cirque of peaks from the ridge south of Broaghnabinnia leading to Stumpa Duloigh and finally swinging southward over to Knocknabreeda.

Continue westward onto an area of broken ground. At **V 805**65 **803**32, you will meet a stream running down the slopes of Broaghnabinnia. Cross this stream and ascend a moderate slope of grass and rock, now in a north-westerly direction, aiming for the ridge line above.

Broaghnabinnia extension: Upon arriving at the stream at **V 805**65 **803**32, you could opt to climb Broaghnabinnia, the mighty rise to the north. It is a punishing slope of 345m height gain and a there-and-back distance of 2km. Add about 1 to 1¼ hours for this extension. The summit is a broad, grassy area marked by some fence posts. The Irish for it is *Bruach na binne* or 'edge of the mountain'. It does feel rather like that, if you care to wander to the northern edge of its broad top, where the views across to the southern end of the MacGillycuddy's Reeks are enticingly good, with Curraghmore Lake sitting under the steep

A view into Cummeenduff Glen and its lakes, with Lough Reagh and Brassel Mountain in sight.

The delightful waterfall at the back of Lough Reagh.

mountainside below. Note that a direct line southward from Broagh-nabinnia's summit to its col at around **V 800**$_{50}$ **807**$_{00}$ should be avoided as the ground is too steep and rocky for a guaranteed safe descent. From the summit, it is best to retrace your steps to the earlier stream.

Follow the predominantly grassy ridge westward, ascending to point 665m. Here, swing left and southward to walk on the undulating ridge high above Lough Duff until meeting an obvious steep section at **V 787**$_{23}$ **796**$_{40}$: a sting in the tail on the ridge. However, there is a worn path leading upward and it should pose no problems. Upon negotiating this steep section, you will arrive at a plaque at **V 788**$_{07}$ **795**$_{42}$ near point 776m.

The views north to the Reeks and Broaghnabinnia are exceptional. The ink-blue waters of Lough Duff dominate the green valley below, and Cummeenduff glen, its lakes and surrounding mountains can be seen in the distant north-east. From the plaque continue south-westward for a distance of 200m on easy ground to point 784m at **V 786**$_{85}$ **793**$_{72}$, where a

The Stumpa Duloigh ridge with Lough Duff below, and the Reeks beyond, as seen from the ridge leading to Knocknabreeda.

fence intersects at a small pile of rocks. This top is known locally as Stumpa Duloigh or 'stump of the black lake'.

Follow a fence that runs south-eastward down a grassy ridge. The fence turns a distinct left just over a kilometre beyond the summit at **V 796**83 **789**08. Follow its line as it leads down the rugged spur, which is initially steep. This puts you on the broad ridge as it rises, falls and rises again to Knocknabreeda. Leave a line of fences to gain its top at **V 814**72 **792**93 which is marked by a rusted metal post on a pile of rocks.

Views to the north and west toward and beyond the wide valley in which the Gearhameen River twists and turns are good. Stumpa Duloigh in particular looks frighteningly impressive, with its steep eastern slopes plummeting down to Lough Duff below.

Follow a line of fences from Knocknabreeda and after about 700m north-eastward, at **V 820**73 **797**46, the fence intersects. The ground ahead rises slightly among some rocks. Turn left here and zigzag north-westward down a steep slope of short grass, scattered rock and splashes of heather. There is a ruined dwelling near the bottom. Aim for the Gearhameen River at around **V 814**37 **803**10. Upon reaching it, cross the river (more like a stream) and pick your way carefully down rock-benches and outcrops to the waterfall at 'the little garden of Eden' earlier in the walk.

Now it is a matter of simply retracing steps back to the start point in the valley below.

Knocklomena–Boughil Ridge

This rugged ridge separated by Lough Fadda offers panoramic views of Iveragh peaks and the landscape around Moll's Gap.

Grade:	4
Distance:	14km (8¾ miles)
Ascent:	1,050m (3,445ft)
Time:	5¼–6½ hours
Map:	OSi 1:50,000 Sheet 78, OSi 1:25,000 Adventure Series *MacGillycuddy's Reeks & Killarney National Park* or Harvey Superwalker 1:30,000 *MacGillycuddy's Reeks & Killarney National Park*

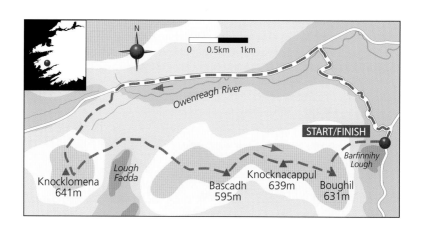

Start/finish: Parking spaces at a lay-by (**V 851**₄₄ **769**₀₅) above Barfinnihy Lough on the R568 from Moll's Gap.

This walk explores four hills west of Moll's Gap: Knocklomena (641m/ 2,103ft), Bascadh (595m/1,952ft), Knocknacappul (639m/2,096ft) and Boughil (631m/ 2,070ft). They are linked by a rugged ridge separated by a broad gap north of Lough Fadda. Also, the descent from Knocklomena down to the gap is steep and on broken ground, and likewise the descent from Boughil to the R568, therefore giving this route a grade of 4. However, the panoramic views of mountains west, north and east more than compensates. This route can also be done in reverse, but then you face a final rise in the road up toward the R568.

Route Description

Head back toward Moll's Gap for about 300m. Turn left on a minor road into the Black Valley. The road winds its way down the slopes north of Boughil. After just over 2km, you arrive at a T-junction at the valley floor.

Take a left at the junction and walk along the minor road just north of the Owenreagh River for a further 3.5km to **V 804**₂₈ **779**₃₄. From here, you should notice a distinct spur rising south-west toward Knocklomena. There is a step-stile at the fence just before a knoll. Go over this stile and ascend a slope of heather and rushes, keeping a fence to your left. Continue southward for a distance of 150m to reach a track, and soon cross another fence ahead.

Keep the fences now to your right and ascend a rugged spur consisting of ling heather, moss and moor grass. Head south-westward, following a faint path in places. After a distance of around 550m up the spur, you will walk along an area of boulders; one in particular is very large. Continue on up, later veering southwards to finally reach the broad top of Knocklomena at **V 797**₄₅ **765**₆₈, marked by a rocky outcrop and a metal post. The panorama of surrounding mountains is magnificent: to the west lie the

The view northwards from Knocklomena toward the Reeks.

Beann range and the pap-like profile of Mullaghan-attin; Ballaghbeama Gap separates it from Knock-aunanattin further east; and the MacGillycuddy's Reeks tower behind the circuit of mountains above the Gearhameen valley to the north. The edge of Lough Brin, whose waters are said to be inhabited by a 'wurrum' – a creature that is either half-fish/half-dragon or half-fish/half-donkey – can be seen in the valley below to the north-west.

The sofa-shaped boulder on the col between Bascadh and Knocknacappul.

From the summit of Knocklomena, descend north-eastward down a steep slope of heather, grass and rocky outcrops. Aim for a broad gap at the northern end of Lough Fadda. Both Lough Fadda and the smaller Lough Beg can be clearly seen on the descent route.

There is a rocky band and grassy ledges just above the gap at **V 805**78 **770**82 where care may be required. The gap can be boggy; walk across it to reach a new fence line at **V 808**78 **771**25.

From here, set a south-eastward course and ascend the rough uneven ground. While you work your way up these slopes, care to look behind at the menacing east face of Knocklomena thrusting skyward from the waters of Lough Fadda. Pick your way through heather-clad knolls and rocky outcrops to emerge somewhere on the grassy ridge, west of point 591m.

There is a line of fences on the ridge. Keep these to your right, and walk to point 591m and summit 595m, which is known locally as Bascadh. The tooth-like profile of Knocknacappul, with the deep clefts that line its western slopes, rises ahead.

The ridge ahead is obvious. Staying close to the fence, descend with care down rocky outcrops and grassy ledges: the going is steep but always manageable. You are heading for the col north-east of Bascadh. At the col around **V 826**91 **768**54, there is a large, sofa-shaped grey boulder that you could recline on while having a snack or a snooze.

Keeping the fence line on your right, ascend the bare rock amongst the grassy and short heather, avoiding some bog pools. Look out for St Patrick's cabbage growing in abundance amongst the rock crevices. There is a faint path as you near the summit of Knocknacappul (*Cnoc na gCapall*, 'hill of the horses') at **V 834**05 **767**28, marked by a pile of rocks arranged around a rusted metal post.

An amazing view awaits you here, especially on a clear day. One is drawn to the breathtaking panorama from the north to the east: from the Reeks, to the Gap of Dunloe, then of Purple Mountain, Torc Mountain and the Mangerton plateau.

Next, descend eastward down a moderate rough slope of grass and rock to the col beyond. At a point where fences intersect, cross it and follow a new fence line, keeping this to your right. The fence intersects

The view from the summit of Boughil: Barfinnihy Lough below, Moll's Gap and the string of hills beyond.

again near the top of Boughil, at a small pile of rocks at **V 841**94 **764**91. Cross this and walk to the summit.

Boughil comes from the Irish *Buachaill,* meaning 'cowherd' or 'herdsman'. It makes me think of those famous mountains in Scotland: the Buachaille Etive Mòr and Buachaille Etive Beag in Glen Coe.

Step close to the eastern edge of Boughil to be greeted by yet another splendid view. Barfinnihy Lough lies sprawled in the barren valley below. The grey ribbon of road can be seen weaving across the brown-yellow landscape toward Moll's Gap. The rough hillside of Derrygarriff rises beyond Moll's Gap, with the rest of the view in the distance similar to that as from Knocknacappul.

Moll Kissane ran a small pub at Moll's Gap when the Killarney–Kenmare road was built in the 1820s. There Moll sold the illicit home-brewed *poitín,* the colourless alcoholic drink distilled from potatoes in pots under moonlight. Its dry, sweet and grainy-flavoured liquid required about seven times its own portion of water to chasten it!

The parking spaces at the start of the walk can also be seen from these heights, as can the descent route.

The descent is rough, steep and uneven: there is much rock to contend with, although it is also grassy in places. Around a distance of 200m north of the summit, you will meet some fences at **V 841**57 **766**68. Follow the line of fences; however, in some places you may need to leave it in order to avoid hazardously steep ground on your right. In essence: pick the safest route that offers the least resistance north-eastward down the slope.

At around **V 846**83 **770**35, veer eastward rejoining the fence again and follow its line, keeping it to your right, to the R568. Upon reaching the road, turn right and walk back to the start point.

The Coomloughra Horseshoe

Climb the three highest peaks in Ireland via airy ridges in this classic mountain horseshoe route.

Grade:	5
Distance:	13.5km (8½ miles)
Ascent:	1,250m (4,101ft)
Time:	6–7 hours, time added for difficulty of terrain
Map:	OSi 1:50,000 Sheet 78, OSi 1:25,000 Adventure Series *MacGillycuddy's Reeks & Killarney National Park* or Harvey Superwalker 1:30,000 *MacGillycuddy's Reeks & Killarney National Park*

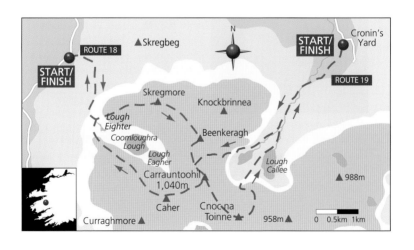

Start/finish: A large, new car park at the base of the Hydro Road at **V 771**₈₃ **871**₁₇. If this car park overflows, then use a large lay-by just over 1km further away on the road toward Lough Acoose at **V 764**₀₀ **865**₀₀.

Note: It is recommended to do the horseshoe in a clockwise direction in case of retreat if one does not like the look of the Beenkeragh arête. An alternative route is a there-and-back from the Hydro Road up to Caher, and then to Carrauntoohil – leaving out the Beenkeragh arête altogether. Take extra care on the exposed ridge in wet or windy conditions. It is not advisable to attempt the ridge in strong winds or gales. Wind speed at cols is greater so take care along sections of the ridge where the path goes over a col. In winter, under snow and ice conditions, this route becomes a serious mountaineering venture requiring the use of crampons and ice axes.

The MacGillycuddy's Reeks are home to nine of the ten highest summits in Ireland, all of which are over 3,000ft. It is a range named after the servant or son of Cuddy, a former local landlord. Of all its summits, Carrauntoohil is the highest. At 1,040m (3,412ft), it is also the highest mountain in Ireland. This classic horseshoe route scales its lofty heights via the airy Beenkeragh ridge and returns by way of Caher, the third highest mountain in Ireland.

The Beenkeragh arête leading to Carrauntoohil.

Route Description

Cross a stile at the rear of the car park near the Mountain Rescue board. Turn right and follow a concrete path, known locally as the Hydro Road, uphill. Underneath, a metre-wide pipe transports water from the lakes above to an electricity generator below.

Follow the Hydro Road as it leads up the hill then later veers southward under the slopes of Breanlee. Cross a bridge over a stream and soon after there is a metal gate as the track veers south-east toward Lough Eighter, the 'lower lake' at **V 777**₆₆ **855**₈₂. The location is an amphitheatre that showcases a view of the entire horseshoe.

A path through slopes of heather ascends quite steeply north-eastward to summit 747m. A band of rock slabs and outcrops guard the summit, which is marked with a cairn. From here, follow the broad crest eastward, then south-east to the summits of Skregmore (848m/2,782ft) – the 'large rocky place' – and Stuaic Bharr na h-Abhann (851m/2,792ft) –the 'stump of the top of the river'. These tops are rocky and stony, both marked with cairns, whereas the cols connecting them are grassy.

The rise to the south-east after the next col is a steep ascent over rocks and boulders to the lofty summit of Beenkeragh (1,010m/3,314ft) at **V 801**$_{23}$ **852**$_{44}$. Its Irish equivalent, *Binn Chaorach,* means 'peak of the sheep'. There are records to show that flocks of sheep replaced the goats that used to graze the area after the Famine. Like its place-name meaning, you might feel a little sheepish looking southward across the narrow, knife-edged ridge that links Beenkeragh to the imposing northern face of Carrauntoohil beyond. South-eastward, the ground falls away steeply to the yawning hollow of Cummeenoughter and the bristly east ridge leading to Stumpa an tSaimh.

A rocky crest leads south-westward from the summit of Beenkeragh to the ridge linking it with Carrauntoohil. Experienced scramblers may choose to take this exposed line, which later meets up with a path along the ridge at around **V 800**$_{19}$ **851**$_{05}$. There is also a faint path to the left just under this crest which eventually leads to the same grid location. However, the feeling of exposure of the plunge toward Cummeenoughter to the left below may not be to everyone's taste.

By far the safest descent from the summit of Beenkeragh is via a prominent, less-exposed path south-westward, to the right and just under its rocky crest on the Coomloughra (western) side. In thick mist, this path is on a bearing of 234° (make appropriate adjustments for magnetic variation). As you descend the steep path, the Coomloughra lakes can be seen below initially, with the rocky crest now just above you to the left. The path soon turns a corner at around **V 800**$_{87}$ **852**$_{26}$, after which there are some short rocky and boulder-strewn sections to negotiate, before it finally drops steeply to the ridge at **V 800**$_{19}$ **851**$_{05}$.

Here, you can afford some respite: a prominent path skirts to the right of a block of rock on the Coomloughra side and heads in a general southward direction. About 100m away, the path approaches a large rock slab and rises slightly to the right of it at around **V 800**$_{01}$ **849**$_{67}$. Keep following this distinct path as it undulates along the ridge, bypassing more rock slabs on the way, before finally arriving at a notch in the ridge at **V 800**$_{68}$ **846**$_{53}$.

A sharp rib of rock looms ahead and above: this is an airy top of the ridge marked as point 959m on OSi maps, or known locally as The Bone. Very experienced scramblers may wish to include this summit, then carefully negotiate a way down steep rocks to the right of it and down (southward) to the col below.

The safest option for walkers, however, is to keep on the narrow path that skirts to the left and under this rocky rib on the eastern side (that facing Carrauntoohil). There is a steep drop (and fine views) toward O'Shea's Gully to the left below. At **V 800**$_{73}$ **846**$_{38}$, ignore the faint path rising to the right. Instead, follow the more prominent path down to the left. This rocky path swings to the right soon after around **V 800**$_{79}$ **846**$_{18}$, and then around a corner amongst rocky terrain under point 959m (which is now above you to your right), leading the walker safely to the col below.

At the col you are on top of O'Shea's Gully. From here, it is a steep ascent south-eastward over more boulders, with St Patrick's Cabbage

The Caher ridge with Lough Eagher, Coomloughra Lough and Lough Eighter below and the Skregmore tops across in the distance.

growing in its rocky crevices. You will pass the tops of two gullies, Central Gully and Curved Gully, below on your left before the slope flattens and veers north-eastward to the summit of Carrauntoohil (1,040m/3,412ft). A stone shelter and a steel cross mark the summit at **V 803**67 **844**25. The cross was erected in 1976 to replace a timber cross before it. Its surface is charred black due to lightning strikes. Here you are above it all and views are all encompassing, including most of the peaks in the south-west of Ireland. Most impressive are views toward the Beenkeragh ridge and to the eastern end of the Reeks in the opposite direction.

In November 2014, the iconic metal cross on Carrauntoohil's summit was cut down by vandals but reinstated by the local community a week later.

From Carrauntoohil's summit, head south-south-west, aiming toward the ridge linking to Caher. Be careful not to descend south-eastward on the Devil's Ladder route, which heads a different direction. Important note: If you come across a 'Turn Back Now' sign you are heading the wrong way. The sign warns walkers off attempting any descent route down the vertiginous east face of Carrauntoohil where a fall is fatal.

There is a fine path along the humpback ridge, nowhere near as narrow as Beenkeragh, toward the summit cairn of Caher (1,001m/3,284ft) at **V 792**60 **838**90. There are fine views of the Coomloughra lakes below on your right as you approach Caher. Caher is also a good place to look across Coomloughra and appreciate the serrated edge of Beenkeragh beyond.

A slight descent downhill leads to a stony and grassy gap. Beyond the stone wall and old fence, a rocky slope leads to the summit cairn of Caher's West Top (975m/3,199ft). From here, descend a moderately steep scree slope for a distance of about 500m, after which it relents and the terrain becomes stony and grassy around **V 786**72 **844**21. Just over a kilometre away, around Lyreboy at **V 777**84 **851**28, come off the spur and descend heathery slopes toward the north-western end of Lough Eighter below. From here, retrace steps along the Hydro Road back to the start.

Carrauntoohil via O'Shea's Gully

An adventurous route to the top of Ireland's highest mountain via a stunning rocky amphitheatre and a steep gully.

Grade:	5
Distance:	12km (7½ miles)
Ascent:	1,000m (3,281ft)
Time:	5–6 hours
Map:	OSi 1:50,000 Sheet 78, OSi 1:25,000 Adventure Series *MacGillycuddy's Reeks & Killarney National Park* or Harvey Superwalker 1:30,000 *MacGillycuddy's Reeks & Killarney National Park*

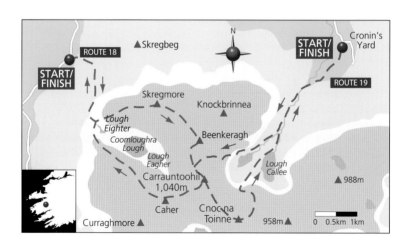

Start/finish: Cronin's Yard at **V 836**₆₅ **873**₄₀.

Note: It is not advisable to attempt this route in strong winds or gales. In winter, under snow and ice conditions, this route becomes a serious mountaineering venture requiring the use of crampons and ice axes.

The MacGillycuddy's Reeks are home to nine of the ten highest summits in Ireland, all of which are over 3,000ft. Carrauntoohil, its highest at 1,040m (3,412ft), is also the highest mountain in Ireland. This approach to the summit of Carrauntoohil is from its northern end, starting from the well-facilitated Cronin's Yard (www.croninsyard.com). A rocky ascent up a series of rock steps enters a stunning rocky amphitheatre at the base of O'Shea's Gully, before the final push up the summit. The return is via the steep but well-trodden mountain path of the Zigzags.

Looking toward Ireland's highest mountains: Carrauntoohil and Beenkeragh as seen from slopes above Meallis.

Route Description

There are a number of plaques on a stone wall opposite the €2 coin-box and house at Cronin's Yard. Walk through a metal gate by a sign that points the way to Carrauntoohil. There are a further two metal gates, one with a swinging metal gate on the right. The broad track passes some gorse bushes, hawthorn and holly trees on the left, and then crosses a stream. It runs along a stony track, passing a patch of spruce and mountain pine on the left.

New metal footbridges have been erected at **V 830**₄₇ **865**₈₆ and **V 828**₇₀ **864**₈₀ over the stream and the Gaddagh River. After crossing the first metal footbridge, the path forks: take the right fork with a sign pointed for 'Carrauntoohil Mountain'. This path takes you to the bridge over the Gaddagh, after then rises to meet the Lisleibane track. Turn left at this track with the river now on your left. The track becomes stony as you walk under a small, crumpled fold of serrated rock above on your right – these are the crags of the Hags Teeth. A larger rocky promontory sits slightly further away – the Large Tooth or *Fiacail Mhór*.

Just before the track crosses the part of the Gaddagh River flowing from Lough Gouragh (*Loch Gabhrach*, 'lake of an area full of sheep') at **V 821**₃₄ **854**₉₃, leave it and veer right to ascend a grassy knoll. There are rocks and boulders splashed on the grassy ground as you pass under the

Large Tooth above on the right. Further ahead, the prominent spike of Stumpa an tSaimh, 'stump of the sorrel' thrusts skyward: a narrow, rocky ridge leads westward from its summit to Beenkeragh.

The new bridge over the Gaddagh River. Carrauntoohil projects skyward, far left.

Remain close to the stream until **V 816**₂₃ **850**₆₂ where a stony path leads uphill. Lough Gouragh now appears beyond the stream, and as height is gained Lough Callee can be seen as well. At **V 813**₁₈ **849**₉₃ the path crosses the stream, which cascades southward from higher slopes. It is a good place to stop for a snack as Carrauntoohil and its Howling Ridge, the crumpled rock of Stumpa an tSaimh and delightful cascades above, the lakes below, and the Reeks ridge all come into view.

The path now rises to meet a series of rock steps known as Na Teanntaí. The first at **V 812**₀₀ **849**₄₆ is a series of rock ledges leading to a grassy and rocky platform above. The second at **V 811**₃₇ **848**₉₉ is a short scramble up rock steps that leads to a rocky ramp around a corner to the left. The third at **V 810**₃₀ **848**₄₀ is a scramble up some rock slabs and steep grass.

Once pass Na Teanntaí, you will arrive at a wide valley surrounded by rocky cliffs and a jagged ridge above on the right. This is the little lower coum of Cummeeneighter at **V 809**₅₁ **848**₄₁. A cascade can be seen plunging down from a higher valley ahead. A worn path under some crags on the left snakes its way up to the higher valley. Walk to the path at **V 807**₀₈ **847**₄₃ which is scree-filled, keep the cascade to your right, and ascend to the small middle coum of Cummeenlour at **V 805**₄₂ **848**₄₆.

As you round a corner here, O'Shea's Gully appears ahead: it is grassier at the top of the gully with scree tumbling to its bottom. There are dark, narrow and steeper gullies to the left of O'Shea's: these are Central Gully and Curved Gully respectively. These were formed due to a geological fault causing a crack in the earth's crust millions of years ago. Carrauntoohil itself is an uplifted fold following an earthquake, but is now a battered stump of its original size after several ice ages.

Follow a path to the left of the cascade to yet another valley – the little upper coum of Cummeenoughter at **V 803**₄₂ **848**₃₂. A lake, the highest in Ireland, sits here, flanked by the vertiginous cliffs of Carrauntoohil and Beenkeragh. From here, veer south-westward and ascend the loose rock and scree of O'Shea's Gully at **V 802**₂₀ **846**₈₃. The steep gully is named after Brother O'Shea who died in 1968 after falling there.

Arrive at the top of the col and ascend to the summit cross of Carrauntoohil as per Route 18. On a clear day from Carrauntoohil you should be able to make out the path of the Zigzags (the descent route) on slopes below Cnoc na Toinne.

From the summit, follow a well-trodden path that leads south-eastward to the top of the Devil's Ladder at **V 806**₈₇ **836**₆₇. Its upper slopes are decorated with sea thrift, whose round-headed flowers glow bright pink in spring. The slope is on loose rock and scree initially, becoming stony and grassier later on a broad gap above the Ladder.

Do not go down the Devil's Ladder but instead ascend south-eastward to the grassy top of Cnoc na Toinne (845m/2,772ft) at **V 811**₁₅

Walkers ascending O'Shea's Gully with Lough Cummeenoughter below.

833₉₉. Walk on its flat plateau for a distance of about 350m to a small pile of rock at **V 813**₈₉ **834**₇₀ that marks the start of the Zigzags, the steep path that leads off the slopes of Cnoc na Toinne to emerge on the valley floor near the base of the Devil's Ladder gully. From the small rock pile, it heads north-eastward, then north-north-west, before turning left at **V 814**₇₅ **840**₈₃.

Now with the Devil's Ladder ahead of you in the distance, keep on the grassy path to around **V 812**₆₃ **840**₂₁ and here descend westward (the Ladder is now to your left) for about 200m to meet a path in the valley below.

The path initially follows a stream on the left then later veers away from it. It leads down into the Hags Glen.

This is where Patrick Weston Joyce, the Irish historian and writer, thought of Carrauntoohil as an 'inverted sickle', perhaps because the distinctive ridges that soar up the mountain's steep face from here resemble the serrated teeth of a saw. Its Irish equivalent is *Corrán Tuathail* or 'Tuathal's sickle', (a sickle is a tool with a curved blade for cutting crops). Tuathal was a popular surname in medieval Ireland.

As you walk comfortably on the well-worn path in the solitude of the Hags Glen think of the poor souls who lived in this rugged valley during the Famine. The glen is also said to be the abode of *An Cailleach*, a powerful Celtic goddess who roams these parts and also crannies on the Beara Peninsula.

The path crosses the Gaddagh River at **V 821**₁₇ **854**₂₀, where you wandered off earlier in the day toward the Large Tooth.

Now retrace earlier steps toward the two footbridges leading back to Cronin's Yard.

Coomloughra Lakes via the Hydro Road

Visit the three lakes of Coomloughra and walk below the cliffs and crags of Ireland's highest mountains.

Grade:	3
Distance:	9km (5½ miles)
Ascent:	400m (1,312ft)
Time:	3–3¾ hours
Map:	OSi 1:50,000 Sheet 78, OSi 1:25,000 Adventure Series *MacGillycuddy's Reeks & Killarney National Park* or Harvey Superwalker 1:30,000 *MacGillycuddy's Reeks & Killarney National Park*

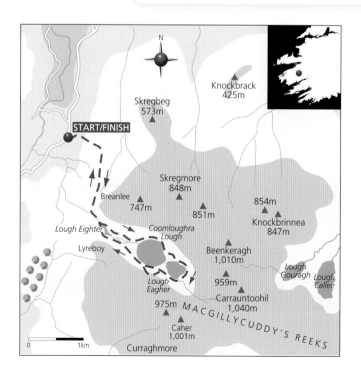

Start/finish: A large, new car park at the base of the Hydro Road at **V 771**₈₃ **871**₁₇. If this car park overflows, then use a large lay-by just over 1km further away on the road toward Lough Acoose at **V 764**₀₀ **865**₀₀.

The high-level circuit of Coomloughra via the Hydro Road is described in Route 18, taking in the three highest mountains in Ireland – Carrauntoohil, Beenkeragh and Caher. This route follows the same Hydro Road to the dam at Lough Eighter. From there, it traces a circuit around the three lakes of Coomloughra. Some scrambling is required on the southern side of the lakes, but this is optional.

Route Description

Cross a stile at the rear of the car park near the Mountain Rescue board. Turn right and follow a concrete path, known locally as the Hydro Road, uphill. The gradient relents after a bend, under the slopes of Breanlee. Reach a concrete bridge after passing through two metal gates. The stream gushing under the bridge is the outflow from Lough Eighter.

Continue steadily uphill to reach the dam on the western end of Lough Eighter. The view across the lough is to an impressive amphitheatre surrounded by a ring of mighty peaks. Cross the outlet stream of Lough Eighter and follow a path along its shoreline, with the lake now to your right.

The path is initially stony then later turns grassy and boggy in places. It continues to the far end of the lake then meanders alongside a stream that connects Lough Eighter to Coomloughra Lough. Keep the stream on the right and follow the path as it turns stony again to reach a grassy knoll near the shoreline of Coomloughra Lough. This is an idyllic spot, with the lake spread out in front and the vertiginous cliffs of Caher behind.

Keeping the lake to your right follow close to its shoreline, passing a stone circle near its midway point at **V 787**₇₅ **853**₁₇. Cross several streams, then followed by a slight rise to reach a flat, boulder-strewn area at

The craggy section above the south-east corner of Coomloughra Lough requires care and a scramble around the outcrop of vertiginous rock.

V 791₅₅ **850**₃₁. This is a point between the lakes of Coomloughra and Eagher which together form an hourglass figure. On days when the water level is high, the lakes become a single entity. The cliffs, crags and gullies of Caher frown down from above its scree-filled slopes.

Continue along the shores of Lough Eagher, keeping it to the right. The steep ground

96

on the left edges closer and almost touches the lake further along its shore. The ground is boulder strewn and has to be negotiated with care. A vague path exists at the far end of Lough Eagher and circles inward, with the lake still to the right. The path gradually rises to reach a flat area at **V 792**99

Lough Eagher and Coomloughra Lough with the Skregmore tops rising on the right.

84642 surrounded by a natural amphitheatre. The place is quiet and has a wild and remote feel to it. The landscape ahead is ringed by a network of crags and cliffs. A stream flows into Lough Eagher from above, tumbling down the rugged slopes which are lined with bands of scree and dotted with rocks and boulders. The view back along Lough Eagher is impressive too, flanked by the dark, steeper, craggy hillside of Caher on the left and the brown-yellow, tamer, grassy slopes of Skregmore on the right.

Descend to cross the stream flowing into Lough Eagher. The next section of the walk involves a traverse on the opposite (southern) side of Lough Eagher and Coomloughra Lough, keeping the lakes on your right at all times.

Pick up a vague path just above the lakeshore of Lough Eagher. The path passes a large outcrop of rock at **V 791**36 **846**01. Around 150m after this outcrop, the path seems to descend steeply through a gap between rock clefts. It is best to avoid this gap, bypassing it by veering left up a slight rise.

The path now becomes more distinct. The going is easy for around 200m but then it reaches its next obstacle at the southern end of Coomloughra Lough. The path descends to meet a large, rocky crag at **V 788**44 **848**14. The aim is to pick a way to the right of this crag near its base and above the lakeshore.

It is an awkward section and you will need to get your hands on rock for some easy 'up' and 'down' scrambling moves. The drop on the right to the lake is quite steep and exposed, so take care. If scrambling is not your cup of tea, bypass this section completely to the left by ascending the steep slope to clear the crag, then descend on its other end to meet a path there.

All difficulties end once this crag is passed. The path improves again briefly and passes a stone circle at **V 785**18 **848**85. After this it deteriorates once again. Walk across trackless moorland which can be boggy in places. Follow a stream and then Lough Eighter on your right, to return to the dam. From there, retrace steps down the Hydro Road back to the start.

The Reeks Ridge

A knife-edge crest, super scrambling and stupendous views are the attractions along the most challenging mountain ridge in Ireland.

Grade:	5
Distance:	9km (5¾ miles)
Ascent:	980m (3,215ft)
Time:	5–6 hours, time added for difficulty of terrain
Maps:	OSi 1:50,000 Sheet 78, OSi 1:25,000 Adventure Series *MacGillycuddy's Reeks & Killarney National Park* or Harvey Superwalker 1:30,000 *MacGillycuddy's Reeks & Killarney National Park*

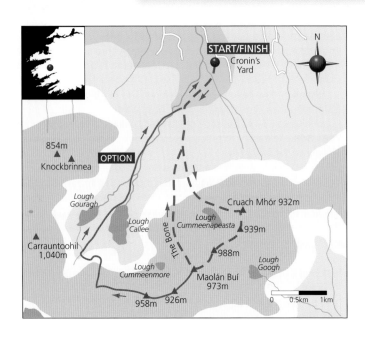

Start/Finish: Cronin's Yard (www.croninsyard.com) at **V 836**65 **873**40.

Note: The summits in this walk are unnamed in the OSi Sheet 78 1:50000 map.

Safety Note: If you suffer from vertigo, or are of nervous disposition, then this walk is **not** for you. Do not attempt this route in strong winds or gales. In winter, and under snow and ice conditions, it is a serious mountaineering venture requiring the use of crampons and ice axes.

The MacGillycuddy's Reeks are also known as *Na Cruacha Dubha*, or 'the black stacks'. One summit in the eastern end of the Reeks is called Cruach Mhór (932m/3,058ft), meaning 'big stack'. The section of ridge from Cruach Mhór over the Big Gun (939m/3,081ft) and to Cnoc na Péiste (988m/3,241ft) is harder than that between Carrauntoohil and Beenkeragh – and in places is knife-edge. The descent route is via a spur off Maolán Buí (973m/3,192ft) called The Bone, a fine way to end the day, as the views across the Hags Glen toward Carrauntoohil and Beenkeragh is rewarding.

Route Description

There are a number of plaques on a stone wall opposite the €2 coin box and house at Cronin's Yard. Walk through a metal gate by a sign that points the way to Carrauntoohil. There are a further two metal gates, one with a swinging metal gate on the right. The broad track passes some gorse bushes, hawthorn and holly trees on the left, and then crosses a stream. It runs along a stony track, passing a patch of spruce and mountain pine on the left.

Veer left at **V 830**45 **865**91 before reaching the new bridge at a stream. Keeping the stream on your right, follow the wooden posts to an aluminium ladder stile about 200m uphill at **V 830**68 **864**09. From here ascend, southeastward up a grassy slope toward Lough Cummeenapeasta above. The slope is scattered with rock and steepens as you gain height. Views across the Hags Glen toward Carrauntoohil, Beenkeragh and Knockbrinnea are good.

You might want to linger awhile upon reaching the dark waters of Lough Cummeenapeasta, the lake of the 'coum of the serpent',

The view eastwards from Carrauntoohil to a section of the Reeks stretching from Cnoc an Chuillinn to Cruach Mhór in the distance.

99

On the summit of the Big Gun looking along its section of ridge toward Cruach Mhór.

where the sheer cliffs at its far end stare down in stark silence. Here, early on 17 December 1943, a DC3 transport plane, flying from Morocco to England and wildly off course, crashed into cliffs above Lough Cummeenapeasta. The conditions were savage at the time and no one even saw or reported the incident. It was not discovered until about a month and a half later.

From the shores of Lough Cummeenapeasta, ascend the steep, rocky slope toward Cruach Mhór (point 932m) in an easterly direction. About halfway up the slope, a boulder field stands between you and the summit. Take your time here, using your hands for balance if necessary. There is interesting flora to spot amongst the boulders in spring: hairy cap moss, star moss, wood rush, St Patrick's cabbage and bright-red Devil's Matchsticks.

Near the summit, a stony path leads to a large stone grotto on top of Cruach Mhór at **V 840**77 **848**23. A man from the townland of Ballyledder to the north-west was said to have hauled plastic bags filled with water from Lough Cummeenapeasta below. Tommy Sullivan laboured for years to bring cement, gravel and water to these heights to build this grotto in the 1970s.

As you now gaze toward the narrow ridge leading from Cruach Mhór over to the Big Gun perhaps, like Tommy, it would be wise to say your prayers.

At the back of the stone grotto (on the opposite side of its niche) is a path leading southward to the ridge that connects Cruach Mhór to the Big Gun. The going gradually becomes rocky as it descends to a path on a broad section of the ridge about 50m away at **V 840**65 **847**68.

Almost immediately after, the ridge ahead becomes a narrow rocky arête and in several places there are large boulders forming slabs and sharp pinnacles, or *gendarmes*. Very experienced scramblers with a head for heights may wish to crest this ridge. However, it is advisable for most walkers to tackle the ridge using the notes that follow: even so, easy scrambling moves are required in sections.

Soon after this broad section, outflank all immediate rock outcrops to its right using vestigial paths under the pinnacles on the Cummeenapeasta (west) side of the ridge. Shortly after, you will encounter a large rocky pinnacle ahead on the left: outflank this by dropping to the right using a path below it around **V 840**55 **846**92. Be careful not to lose too much height. As soon as you are directly under the pinnacle, carefully scramble up a short distance to regain the ridge.

This brings you to a notch in the ridge between two pinnacles at **V 840**$_{59}$ **846**$_{44}$. Outflank this also to the right, passing a large spear-like rock pointed downwards. Scramble to the left of this projection and then head close to the crest of the rocky ridge, keeping any further pinnacles to the left. At **V 840**$_{61}$ **846**$_{16}$, veer right to outflank the remaining large rocky pinnacles before the summit. Look out for a path slightly lower below, and follow this to a rock step which has to be negotiated in order to reach the summit.

If you cannot surmount this rock step, then drop down slightly lower still to about **V 840**$_{51}$ **845**$_{96}$ and follow a faint path to about **V 840**$_{39}$ **845**$_{63}$. Turn left here to ascend a steep path of scree just to the right of a rocky rib.

Either way, you will eventually reach a path just below the summit of the Big Gun. The final few metres are an obvious rocky scramble to the exposed summit which you must undertake with care. If you do not like the look of this direct southward approach, there are faint paths that branch off to the right just below the summit, which may offer some easier scrambling lines to it.

A small cairn graces the rocky, elevated, table-sized summit at **V 840**$_{68}$ **845**$_{03}$. There are stunning views back to Cruach Mhór, down to Lough Cummeenapeasta, across to Carrauntoohil and also along the next section of ridge leading to Cnoc na Péiste.

It is common to see birds of prey like falcons and kestrels gracing the skies. In the early 19th century, a Dublin-born artist, explorer and writer by the name of Isaac Weld was led by local guides to these lofty heights and witnessed a dozen eagles hovering by. Weld stood on the Big Gun's summit on what he and his guides thought was Carrauntoohil at that time.

Weld writes of the ridge leading to this summit being so narrow that they could 'drop stones into its depths from each hand simultaneously'. Weld then noticed a higher peak ahead, but his guides convinced him otherwise, citing that the knife-edge ridge was impassable. This is where you get the chance to prove Weld's guides wrong. A rocky spur from the Big Gun leads to a grassy gap. Beyond the gap is the knife-edge section of the ridge leading to Cnoc na Péiste (narrower even than the Beenkeragh arête). Here you have the choice: on calm days, the more experienced among you might want to try a purist's traverse over its arête. However, others would be glad to know that there is a rocky path outflanking the ridge top.

One word of warning before you leave the summit of the Big Gun: on misty days, be very careful to take the right spur off its summit – at all costs, do **not** wander down the south-east spur!

Descend steeply with care south-westward, down a rocky section that leads to a col at **V 839**$_{82}$ **843**$_{53}$. Keep to the Lough Googh (south) side, just under the rocky spur (which should be to your right): this is handy on windy days or should you feel exposed along this section. From the col, ascend a slight rise. When the obvious narrow arête looms ahead just after, keep left along an obvious path.

This path skirts under the sharp crest of Cnoc na Péiste, now just above you on the right. You should find yourself on the Lough Googh (southern) side along this path and **not** on the Cummeenapeasta (northern) side. Follow this path, which is intermittent at times, and occasionally rocky and boulder-strewn in places to around **V 837**$_{21}$

Looking towards Carrauntoohil and Beenkeragh from The Bone. Lough Callee and Lough Gouragh sit in the Hags Glen below.

842$_{35}$, where it veers right and climbs steeply to gain the ridge line.

At the top of the ridge line, follow the straightforward path to the summit of Cnoc na Péiste. The view back along its narrowest section toward the Big Gun and Cruach Mhór beyond is one of the finest mountain vistas in Ireland. The summit of Cnoc na Péiste ('Hill of the serpent') is merely a pile of rocks at **V 835**$_{89}$ **841**$_{76}$.

All difficulties are over after Cnoc na Péiste. Drop down to a grassy gap and stroll along the cushiony ridge to the flat, yellow hill of Maolán Buí, also marked by a pile of rock at **V 832**$_{13}$ **838**$_{14}$.

Cnoc an Chuillin Variation: From Maolán Buí, it is possible to continue on the ridge to Cnoc an Chuillin (the 'hill of the rolling incline'). Gentle stony slopes lead down to a grassy ridge, going over summit 926m and then to the cairn of Cnoc an Chuillin (958m/3,143ft) at **V 823**$_{41}$ **833**$_{38}$. Beyond this, a long descent down stony slopes leads to a grassy col, followed by a slight rise to a grassy section. You will then reach the top of the Zigzags at **V 813**$_{89}$ **834**$_{70}$. Descend the Zigzags as per the route description in Route 19. For the extension, it adds only about 3km (2 miles) to the overall route. However, there is an additional 150m (492ft) of total height gain. Add about 1 to 1½ hours to the overall walking time.

Descend north-westward down The Bone: be careful not to tend toward a path that leads to the Hags Glen. A rusted metal post a distance of about 150m from the summit at **V 831**$_{46}$ **839**$_{65}$ confirms your direction. The view westward is engaging: the moth-like shapes of Lough Callee and Lough Gouragh sit in the Hags Glen, below Ireland's highest mountains.

Lower down, the spur splits into two directions. Descend the spur heading northward at **V 828**$_{51}$ **844**$_{68}$. It is a rocky and rugged descent to a grassy broad spur. Cross a stream at **V 828**$_{92}$ **850**$_{35}$ lower down. Follow the stream, keeping it to the left. Descend the slopes to at last reach the ladder stile crossed earlier and then from there it is a simple trot back to Cronin's Yard.

Lough Acoose to Kate Kearney's Cottage

Follow this classic long-distance route through some of mid-Kerry's most spectacular glens and mountain passes.

Grade:	2/3
Distance:	25km (15½ miles) from Lough Acoose B&B
Ascent:	600m (1,969ft)
Time:	7¼–9¼ hours
Map:	OSi 1:50,000 Sheet 78, OSi 1:25,000 Adventure Series *MacGillycuddy's Reeks & Killarney National Park* or Harvey Superwalker 1:30,000 *MacGillycuddy's Reeks & Killarney National Park*

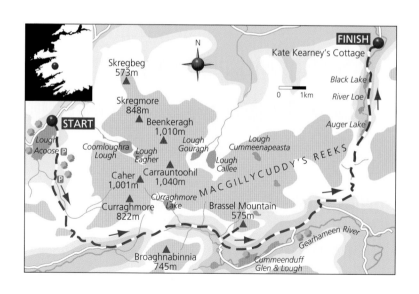

Start: At Lough Acoose which can be approached via minor roads from Killorglin or Beaufort. There are three options for parking near the lake: (1) if staying there, at Lough Acoose B&B (**V 759**$_{67}$ **860**$_{56}$), located near the junction at the northern end of the lake. (2) Drive along a boreen on the eastern end of the lake toward Derrynafeana for around 1.5km (1 mile) to reach a lay-by at a small quarry at **V 761**$_{54}$ **848**$_{12}$. (3) Continue for another 800m from the quarry to reach a fork at **V 761**$_{06}$ **839**$_{86}$ where there are spaces for 2 cars. **Finish:** At the large car park at Kate Kearney's Cottage at **V 881**$_{11}$ **887**$_{96}$ south of Beaufort.

The 214km (133-mile) Kerry Way is one of the most popular long-distance walking trails in Ireland. It is waymarked by Yellow Man signposts and covers some of the most spectacular scenery that the kingdom of Kerry has to offer. This route traces a memorable section of the Kerry Way across the beautiful and lonely glens of Derrynafeana, Bridia and Cummeenduff. Cross some mountain passes in the process, and enjoy spectacular high-level views of the surrounding landscape. The arduous length of 25km (15½ miles) may be split into two days by camping in the wilds or staying at B&Bs or the hostel in the Black Valley, before finishing via the Gap of Dunloe. The grade of 2/3 is given primarily due to its length. The entire route follows boreens, mountain paths and surfaced roads, with the exception of the Brassel and Curraghmore Lake extensions.

Looking north along the Kerry Way above the Gearhanagour Stream at Derrynafeana.

Route Description

Assuming you are starting at Lough Acoose B&B, turn left at the junction by the lake and follow a boreen along its eastern end. Go through a metal gate and walk along the boreen with Lough Acoose (*Loch an Chuais*, 'lake of the recess') on the right. The road follows electric lines and passes a small quarry. It then meanders for around 800m, passing an ancient field system, some houses and under the cover of trees to reach a fork by a conifer patch.

Take the right fork and cross a bridge just after. Pass the ruins of a house on the right and go through a metal gate. Continue ahead at a junction following Kerry Way signposts and pass a farmhouse. The path follows a stone wall, then winds along the wide U-shaped

Looking down on the Bridia valley from the top of the pass flanked by steep slopes of Broaghnabinnia (left) and Curraghmore (right).

valley of Derrynafeana (*Doire na Feinne*, 'oakwood of the Fianna') with the Gearhanagour stream (*Gaortha na Gabhar*, 'woodland of the goats') on the left. The valley is surrounded by steep hillside on three sides, particularly to the east, where the hulking Caher massif casts its shadow on the valley floor. Feral goats are commonly spotted in this secluded valley, which is known in folklore to be the deer-hunting ground for the mythical Fianna and their giant wolfhounds.

Follow the path to the end of the valley then veer right before reaching the spot where the Gearhanagour stream meets the Cummeenacappul stream (*Coimín na gCapall*, 'small coum of the horses'). The signposted path zigzags uphill to reach a fence on a wide, grassy col. The col is a good vantage point to observe the entire length of the Gearhanagour stream as it flows toward the tiny Lough Beg and the blue plate of Lough Acoose in the distance. Continue along the col to reach a stile at **V 767**$_{62}$ **820**$_{52}$ that crosses into the Bridia valley.

The Bridia is one of the most impressive valleys on the Iveragh Peninsula and extends for nearly 7km (4½ miles) from Shronahiree West to Maghanlawaun East. The River Caragh twists and turns along the length of the valley, ultimately flowing into Lough Caragh at Glencar (see Route 11).

Follow signposts and descend down the hillside along a switchback path known as the Lack Road (*Leac*, 'flagstone'). This is an old road used for transporting small kegs of butter or for droving cattle to the market and fairs of Killorglin. There are excellent views down into the Bridia valley, particularly the stretch of hillside from Knockaunanattin to Broaghnabinnia. Looking back, Cloon Lough is also visible away to the west.

Cross some stiles to emerge on a narrow lane by a house in the Bridia Valley at Maghanlawaun (*Macha an Leamhain*, 'milking place of the elms'). Turn left and follow the lane for around 1km to reach a metal gate at **V 788**$_{71}$ **817**$_{43}$. The conical shape of Broaghnabinnia features prominently at the end of the Bridia, with its imposing slopes watching over the silent valley.

Turn left immediately after the metal gate and follow Kerry Way

The view east into Cummeenduff Glen with the Reeks on the left and Brassel Mountain in the distance.

signposts up a ladder stile into a field. Ascend the grassy slope until the path contours along the hillside above a bungalow and a farmhouse below to the right. The townland here is Cappeenthlarig (*Ceapaigh an Chlaraigh*, 'patch of level ground'). Cross another ladder stile by a copse of trees and pass a ruined building on the right.

The path crosses a small stream before passing a stone wall to reach a metal bridge at another stream. A ladder stile beyond the stream leads to a field separated by a bank of stone walls on a grassy slope. Cross another ladder stile by a metal gate on the far end of the field and reach a ruined building. When the path forks, veer left uphill, following the Kerry Way signpost and Yellow Man symbol. Do not follow the Bridia Way sign or Red Man symbol.

The hillside is littered with patches of bracken and scattered rock. Follow the signposts uphill to reach a complex col. At the lip of the col, there are immense views along the length of the Bridia. The name *Na Braighde* or 'the prisons' fits the bill as the narrow glen is guarded by the rocky Caher massif on the right and the imposing slabs of Broaghnabinnia on the left.

After a signpost by some large boulders, the ground begins to flatten along the broad col. Look out for St Patrick's Cabbage within rock crevices along the col. The path meets a ladder stile by a fence at **V 799**₄₁ **821**₇₇ at Curraghmore (*Currach Mhor*, 'big marsh'). Go over the stile and continue along a flat, grassy section before reaching a signpost pointing down into the Cummeenduff Valley at **V 800**₉₉ **821**₃₃. For wild camping enthusiasts, there is a good location for pitching a tent around 500m to the north-east by the outlet of a stream flowing from Curraghmore Lake. If not, veer left and descend toward a yellow house in the valley below.

The Kerry Way contours along the hillside just above the Cummeenduff River and eventually meets a boreen heading east toward Dromluska, below the southern slopes of Brassel Mountain. Near a farmhouse at Dromluska, ignore a junction to the right and continue ahead on the track as the Kerry Way undulates on the hillside above the two lakes of Cummeenduff Glen. The stony path meanders through the deciduous woodland, filled with holly and pine trees.

Brassel Mountain Extension: Brassel Mountain (575m/1,886ft) is a subsidiary top on the southern end of the Reeks offering magnificent views of the mighty Broaghnabinnia. The views from its summit include a sweeping vista of the Reeks to the north, across the Black Valley toward the Upper Lake to the east, and down into Cummeenduff Glen to the south. To climb it, veer left toward open hillside around 150m after the Kerry Way crosses the Glaslhaknockbrossel Stream at **V 821**₅₀ **818**₀₀. Pass a stone circle enclosure then ascend the bracken-laden slopes with the Glaslhaknockbrossel stream now to your left. The terrain is a mix of short grass, rock and scattered boulders. The route ahead is obvious, and you may follow the stream and then veer right, or trace a direct line up steeper ground toward the summit. From the summit, retrace steps back to the Kerry Way below. Additional distance: 2km, ascent: 430m, time: 1½–2 hours.

Somewhere above and between the two lakes, the Kerry Way reaches a metal gate at **V 837**₄₀ **816**₇₁ by some trees at Cloghernoosh (*Clochar Nuis*, 'rock of the new milk'). Go through more metal gates and zigzag downhill by some abandoned houses and stone walls to reach a farmhouse. Veer right at the farmhouse and follow a boreen for around a kilometre until reaching a downhill junction on the right. Folklore has it that the cliffs by a waterfall on your left mark the resting place of the last Viking, buried with his stock of gold.

Ignore the downhill junction and continue ahead to pass Shamrock B&B on the left. Arrive at another junction and veer left there to leave the Kerry Way. Follow a narrow road as it zigzags uphill to reach the Head of Gap. This is a scenic stretch providing stunning views down to the Black Valley on the right.

From the Head of Gap, walk along the Gap of Dunloe to reach Kate Kearney's Cottage. This section of the walk is described in detail in Route 23.

Looking down on the Black Valley from the road leading up to the Head of Gap.

Tomies, Shehy and Purple Mountain

An excellent circuit over three distinctive summits and through a famed glacial valley.

Grade:	4
Distance:	18km (11¼ miles)
Ascent:	820m (2,690ft)
Time:	6–7½ hours
Map:	OSi 1:50,000 Sheet 78, OSi 1:25,000 Adventure Series *MacGillycuddy's Reeks & Killarney National Park* or Harvey Superwalker 1:30,000 *MacGillycuddy's Reeks & Killarney National Park*

Start/finish: A large car park at Kate Kearney's Cottage (**V 881**₁₁ **887**₉₆) south of Beaufort.

The Gap of Dunloe is a lake-filled and ice-sculpted valley from the glacial ages. A narrow road twists its way through the rocky gap whose walls consist of vertiginous crags and sheer cliffs, a haven for rock climbers. It is one of Ireland's famed beauty spots where throngs of tourists visit to take a stroll or a jaunting-car ride. This rugged, high-level route takes us above the eastern flanks of the Gap of Dunloe, over Tomies Mountain (735m/2,411ft), Shehy Mountain (762m/2,500ft) and Purple Mountain (832m/2,730ft), before returning via the road that cuts through Gap.

Auger Lake and the Gap of Dunloe from the northern slopes of Tomies Mountain.

Route Description

Kate Kearney's Cottage, now a pub and restaurant, was once where *poitín* was brewed in the 1840s. *Poitín* is an alcoholic drink distilled from potatoes. The intoxicating brew at the cottage was called 'Kate Kearney's Mountain Dew', and was illegally sold there at the time.

Head north up the road away from Kate Kearney's and the Gap of Dunloe. Pass Moriarty's on the left and cross a concrete bridge over the River Loe. Look out for a double metal gate at **V 881**₄₃ **894**₁₆ on the right shortly after passing Bugler's Cottage.

Go through the metal gate on the right (do not take the one on the left – that leads to a field). Continue to a bend and veer left there, ignoring the metal gate in front. Follow the track running between the trees and with a ditch on the left. Veer right shortly at a bend and keep following the track for another 300m to reach a metal gate. The track passes a large field enclosed by a wooden fence on the right.

Glas Lough: the descent route runs along the right of the lake before descending south-westward beyond.

Go through the gate and continue to reach a T-junction where Lough Leane comes into sight. Turn right there to meet a fence corner at **V 888**₁₆ **892**₇₈. Follow the fence southward and uphill on slopes of bracken, grass and heather. Continue for around 2km to reach a shoulder above Tomies Rock – an outcrop of conglomerate rock with gaunt gullies and vertical chimneys. A route up one of its chimneys is known as *Céim an Fhia* or 'leap of the deer', after mythical tales of deer jumping from there over the Gap of Dunloe.

Veer south-eastwards along the spur on a grassy and heathery slope to reach a pile of rock at point 568m. From here, the scree-covered slopes of Purple Mountain can be seen gleaming in purple hues, lending the mountain its name. The monstrous size of Lough Leane also dominates the plains of Killarney to the east.

Follow the stony path south-eastward, which becomes rocky near the summit of Tomies Mountain (*Na Tóimí*, 'burial ground') at **V 895**₂₆ **867**₇₈. The summit is marked by a string of cairns and a stone shelter. There are fine views across the Gap of Dunloe toward the eastern end of the MacGillycuddy's Reeks.

Looking northward along the Gap of Dunloe with Auger Lake in view and Tomies Mountain rising to the right.

110

Descend southward from the summit toward a broad grassy col. A stony ridge leads to a cairn on the rocky, subsidiary summit of point 757m. From there, head south-eastwards and then dogleg to the summit of Shehy Mountain at **V 901**79 **857**06. There is no need to re-ascend point 757m on your return, rather just contour below its southern slopes and rejoin the main route.

The main route leads south-westwards along a rocky ridge before a steep incline culminates in a string of cairns at **V 886**38 **851**68, marking the summit of An Sliabh Corcra or Purple Mountain. The views from here are the best of the route, with the mighty Reeks and all of the mountains surrounding the Black Valley and Cummeenduff now visible.

From Purple Mountain, descend carefully over boulders and rocks to point 793m. Glas Lough, the 'green lake', can be seen in the rugged hillside below. Descend the spur southward on loose rock and heather. The ground turns grassier before flattening at **V 880**77 **845**28. A rocky path veers to the right here, marked by rusted metal posts, to reach Glas Lough below.

Glas Lough sits in a rugged enclave fringed by crags on its eastern end. With the lake and crags to your left, descend south-westward along an informal path to reach a grassy area and cross a stream at **V 876**34 **840**34. Keep the stream to your left and follow rusted metal posts and a stone wall. After around 300m, the path veers right and descends toward the Head of Gap below. A large rock slab sliced in two, known as Madman's Rock, sits nearby at **V 873**68 **836**97, for those curious enough to visit.

On reaching the Head of Gap, turn right and walk along the Gap of Dunloe. Follow in the footsteps of 19th-century explorers, historians, novelists and poets like Macaulay, Scott, Thackeray and Tennyson. The narrow road twists through the Gap, passing a splurge of rhododendron thickets. Pass a ruined house by a clump of woodland and various fields with livestock. The gap is flanked by sheer, vertiginous crags and cliffs that almost touch at a V-shaped notch near Black Lough. Large boulders or erratics were transported by glacial action and deposited by the lake.

Cross two bridges after a bend along a narrow section of road. The V-shaped valley to the north of the Gap soon comes into view below. The road descends by the larger Auger Lake to the left and passes another three lakes before leading downhill to Kate Kearney's.

Strickeen, the Eastern Reeks and Drishana

Explore the heights of the western end of the Gap of Dunloe in this rugged circuit.

Grade:	4
Distance:	16km (10 miles)
Ascent:	810m (2,657ft)
Time:	5½–6¾ hours
Map:	OSi 1:50,000 Sheet 78, OSi 1:25,000 Adventure Series *MacGillycuddy's Reeks & Killarney National Park* or Harvey Superwalker 1:30,000 *MacGillycuddy's Reeks & Killarney National Park*

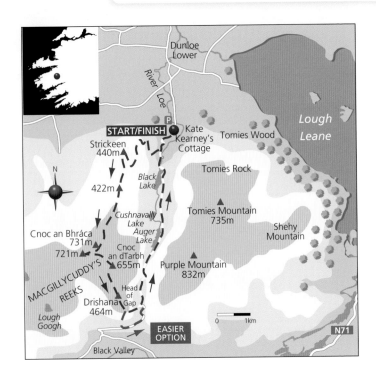

Start/finish: A large car park at Kate Kearney's Cottage (**V 881**₁₁ **887**₉₆) south of Beaufort.

This route explores the hillside on the western end of the Gap of Dunloe. The track leading up to Strickeen (440m/1,443ft) at the start is straightforward, and this Grade 2 summit can be climbed for its own sake for beginners. However, the more experienced could continue southward to bag the three summits of Cnoc an Bhráca (731m/2,398ft), Cnoc na dTarbh (655m/2,149ft) and Drishana (464m/1,522ft) before returning via the Gap of Dunloe.

Looking toward the Reeks from the summit of Strickeen.

Route Description

From Kate Kearney's Cottage, head south toward the Gap of Dunloe. Pass Strickeen House and thereafter the road winds uphill after a sharp bend. As the road straightens, a broad track appears on the right by a Mountain Rescue board on a rock slab at **V 877**₄₃ **882**₉₅.

Leave the road and follow the grassy, stony and rocky track uphill. The track zigzags uphill to reach a flat area on a broad shoulder. The track dwindles to a path and veers right at **V 868**₅₃ **878**₆₄ toward Strickeen (point 440m on the map). Follow the grassy, peaty and intermittent path which becomes rocky nearer the summit. Pass two rocky mounds before reaching a large beehive cairn at **V 866**₃₂ **882**₄₉.

Strickeen is a great vantage point from which to admire the expansive plains to the north between Killorglin and Killarney, and the outflow of the River Laune out to sea. There is also a magnificent view west along the length of the MacGillycuddy's Reeks.

Descend southward from Strickeen and negotiate a boggy patch to reach a fence on the shoulder. The fence heads south along a broad spur leading up to Ballagh Pass. Around 1.5km further along the spur, you will meet a newly erected barbed-wire fence at **V 861**₇₂ **861**₃₀, blocking the way to the main track ahead. Until a stile is installed, do not cross the fence. Instead, keep it on your left and follow it as it doglegs on the slopes below the spur. After around 200m, the fence veers left and rises to meet the main track along the spur once again.

Follow the rocky path to reach the beehive cairn of Cnoc an Bhráca ('hill of the rough ground') at **V 858**₅₉ **854**₆₇. Hop over the fence beyond the cairn, and a stroll of around 400m leads to its subsidiary top, point 721m, marked by moss-covered stone. Here, the narrow ridge rising to the big stack of Cruach Mhór and the jagged arête of rock from there to the Big Gun may be observed at close quarters. Carrauntoohil and the ridge connecting

Looking down on the Gap of Dunloe from the descent route off Drishana toward the Head of Gap.

it to Beenkeragh rise beyond the Hags Glen in the background.

Contour east from point 721m, then descend south-eastward, following an indistinct path toward a saddle below. From the saddle, ascend a grassy and mossy slope to reach a jumble of boulders on the summit of Cnoc na dTarbh ('hill of the bulls', point 655m on the map) at **V 862**₄₁ **850**₀₀. There is small cairn on a rocky area near the summit.

From there, descend south/south-east toward Drishana (point 464m on map). This is a rough stretch with an intermittent path in places but is mainly on peaty and tussocky moorland. As you descend the slope look right for impressive views of the east face of the Big Gun/Cnoc na Péiste massif and Lough Googh on the right. The area near the lake houses some debris of a Douglas C-47 aircraft which crashed in December 1943.

Drishana is gained after a slight rise and its top is marked by a rib of rock. This is where complications begin as the descent to the Head of Gap is testing. Descend the rugged spur south-eastwards, zigzagging down grassy and rocky ramps to avoid a band of cliffs. Meet a fence around 350m further at **V 866**₉₁ **835**₉₉. Veer left and follow the fence initially, by keeping it to your right. When the ground steepens slightly further at **V 868**₇₀ **837**₀₉, veer left again and away from the fence to zigzag down grassy and rocky ramps to avoid cliffs ahead. There are sections where you may have to get hands on rock before meeting the fence again at **V 869**₀₅ **837**₀₉. Avoid steeper ground to the left and using the fence as a guide, descend along a grassy and rocky rib to reach the Head of Gap.

Easier option during the Drishana descent: Upon reaching the fence at **V 866**₉₁ **835**₉₉, veer right and descend the slopes southward (i.e. in the direction of the Black Valley) to meet the road below. Although steep, the slope is easier than the rocky descent to the Head of Gap. It is a kilometre further, however, adding around 20 minutes of walking time. On reaching the road, take a left and continue uphill to reach the Head of Gap. Continue from there down the Gap of Dunloe back to Kate Kearney's Cottage.

Turn left at the Head of Gap and head down the Gap of Dunloe back to Kate Kearney's Cottage. This section of the walk is described in detail in Route 23.

Torc Mountain

Experience one of Kerry's finest panoramas and a 20m waterfall on this well-graded trail.

Grade:	2
Distance:	9km (5½ miles)
Ascent:	500m (1,640ft)
Time:	3–4 hours
Map:	OSi 1:50,000 Sheet 78, OSi 1:25,000 Adventure Series *MacGillycuddy's Reeks & Killarney National Park* or Harvey Superwalker 1:30,000 *MacGillycuddy's Reeks & Killarney National Park*

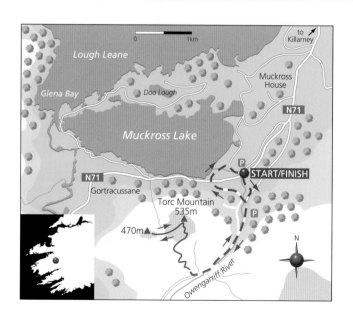

Start/finish: Drive along the N71 from Killarney toward Kenmare and pass the main gate for Muckross House and Gardens on the right. After another 1.7km (1 mile) or so, arrive at the Torc Waterfall car park on the left at **V 965**77 **847**82. The route can also be shortened by around 1.5km (1 mile) by starting at the car park at Cloghereen Upper at **V 967**00 **842**30. However, doing so means omitting Torc Waterfall from the itinerary.

L ocated in the heart of Killarney National Park, the compact summit of Torc Mountain (535m/1,755ft) is a viewpoint not to be missed. All three of the Killarney Lakes and nearly all of Iveragh's chain of peaks form the mother of all panoramas. A fine woodland trail and a well-constructed mountain boardwalk make this route suitable as a family hike or for beginners. Thrown in the mix also is a visit to one of Kerry's most celebrated waterfalls. Note: In winter, the boardwalk leading to Torc Mountain can be icy and treacherous so care is needed.

Route Description

Follow signs for Torc Waterfall from the car park. A firm, wide footpath runs through the native woodlands by a river running along its right. Follow the footpath for around 200m to reach a viewing area at the base of Torc Waterfall. The waterfall is about 20m/66ft high and cascades over rocky shelves to meet the boulder-strewn riverbed below.

The footpath veers left here and ascends steeply up stone slabs through moss- and fern-covered woodlands. It contours along the wooded hillside after a

Torc Waterfall.

bend and passes above a steep, vegetated ravine. Slightly further, it meets a T-junction at **V 966**55 **842**41. Turn left at the T-junction, following signs for 'Kerry Way to Kenmare' or 'Kerry Way to Black Valley'.

Around 50m after, the footpath meets a surfaced road at a T-junction, with a large car park on the opposite end. Turn right there and follow the Yellow Man signpost. Pass a forest barrier with a Wildlife Refuge signboard around 200m further, then continue ahead for another 50m to reach a fork at **V 966**54 **841**32.

Looking toward Torc West Top and the mountains of Iveragh beyond from Torc Mountain.

Take the right fork there. The road now reduces to a track and crosses Torc Old Bridge over the Owengarriff River. Take a left at the T-junction after the bridge and follow the Yellow Man signpost. The track passes another Wildlife Refuge signboard and leads uphill through deciduous woodland, whose floor is extensively carpeted with moss as well as moss-covered rocks. The Owengarriff River flows at the bottom of a steep drop on your left. The ground flattens at the end of the woods and then the track undulates below the southern flanks of Torc Mountain. It passes a vast expanse of rugged moorland to the left, a habitat to the wild deer.

Around 300m after the last trees, reach a path on the right at **V 957**31 **830**40. There is a signboard with the words 'Torc Mountain Footpath: Please Keep To Pathway To Prevent Erosion'. The footpath is made up of a combination of a wire-meshed wooden boardwalk and large stone slabs. It zigzags up to the summit of Torc Mountain (*Sliabh Torc*, 'mountain of wild boar') and conveniently bypasses the bog, gorse, tussocks and rocks that line the slopes.

The view from its summit is stupendous. The massive Lough Leane is visible to the north, along with the myriad of small- to medium-sized islands that dot its waters. The smaller Doo Lough sits between Lough Leane and Muckross Lake, and all the intricacies of Muckross House and its grounds can be observed. Killarney and its vast plains sweep behind the lakes to the north. In every other direction from Torc summit, the view is dominated by mountainous landscape: Shehy, Purple and Tomies Mountains; the MacGillycuddy's Reeks and a host of Iveragh peaks to the west; the wild expanses of Mangerton and Knockrower to the south; Stoompa and Crohane to the east.

Lough Leane, Shehy Mountain and Tomies Mountain from Torc Mountain.

Torc West Top Extension: Peak baggers may wish to descend south-westward to a saddle and then ascend westward to reach the summit of Torc West Top (470m/1,542ft). Add a distance of 1.5km, an ascent of 40m and about 45 minutes' walking time for this extension. On the return, there is no need to climb the main summit again, rather contour along the rugged hillside on its southern flanks to rejoin the boardwalk path at some point. The extension covers mainly trackless ground and has a Grade 3 rating.

Retrace steps from the summit back to the signboard and junction in the woods at **V 966**₅₅ **842**₄₁. Instead of turning right here for the waterfall, continue straight ahead and follow the Yellow Trail over a bridge. Cross the bridge to reach a T-junction.

Turn right and descend down the woodland trail with mountain and lake views occasionally appearing through gaps in the trees. The track bends right slightly further and eventually meets the N71.

Cross the N71 and walk to the rear of the car park on its opposite end to meet a trail signposted 'Muckross House and Torc Waterfall'. Muckross Lake can be seen directly ahead. Turn right here and follow the trail. Walk through a wooded area, with the lake now to your left. The trail passes a large house on the right and reaches a wooden and metal gate at **V 963**₂₂ **847**₈₇.

Ignore the wooden gate on the right and go through the metal gate on the left. Cross a bridge and turn right soon after to follow signs for Torc Waterfall. The tail end of the Owengarriff River flows into Muckross Lake on the right. Veer right before reaching the N71 and follow a footpath under the arch of a bridge to arrive back at the Torc Waterfall car park.

Muckross Lake Loop

An easy loop, suitable for all abilities, around one of Killarney's celebrated lakes.

Grade:	1
Distance:	10km (6¼ miles)
Ascent:	80m (262ft)
Time:	2½–3½ hours
Map:	OSi 1:50,000 Sheet 78, OSi 1:25,000 Adventure Series *MacGillycuddy's Reeks & Killarney National Park* or Harvey Superwalker 1:30,000 *MacGillycuddy's Reeks & Killarney National Park*

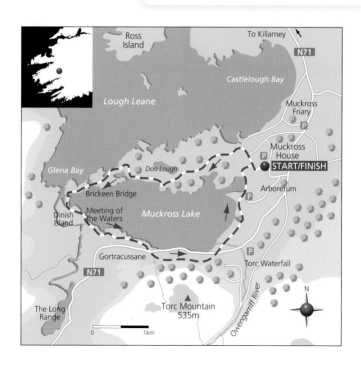

Start/finish: From Killarney town centre, drive along the Kenmare road (N71) for around 6km (3¾ miles). Turn right into Muckross House and Gardens via a large gated entrance, a short distance beyond Muckross Park Hotel. Drive into the grounds and park at the large car park at **V 969**₅₅ **862**₁₀. Note that the automatic gates shut approximately 45 minutes after closing times of Muckross House and the Traditional Farms. For up-to-date information, see: www.muckross-house.ie and www.killarneynationalpark.ie

M uckross Lake is part of the 10,289-hectare Killarney National Park, which contains the largest area of native woodland in Ireland. The woodland is largely comprised of native oak, but there are also yew, birch, hazel, ash, willow and the rare strawberry tree. At its core is the 4,300-hectare Bourn Vincent Memorial Park which was presented to the Irish State in 1932 by Mr and Mrs W. B. Bourn and their son-in-law Senator Arthur Bourn Vincent. In 1981, the Park was designated a Biosphere Reserve by UNESCO. This easy route, almost entirely on tarmac, traces a loop around Muckross Lake, one of the three celebrated Killarney lakes. You might want to include a visit to the house, its craft shop, gardens and traditional farms too.

Colleen Bawn Rock on Muckross Lake, with Eagles Nest and Shehy Mountain in the background.

Route Description

There is an information board giving a map of the grounds at the entrance of the car park and near the public toilets. Veer left on a footpath at the board and then veer right shortly after to follow a signpost for 'Muckross House & Gardens' and 'National Park'.

Muckross House, completed in 1843, is a period-style Victorian mansion close to the shores of Muckross Lake. Built for Henry Arthur Herbert and his wife, this was the fourth house that the Welsh Herbert family had occupied at Muckross over 200 years. In 1770, the Herberts inherited the large estates of the McCarthy family in Killarney.

The footpath crosses a green lawn and passes the Rolf Hook 'Heart/ Butterfly' sculpture on the left. It then leads to the side of Muckross House by a wide green lawn on the right. Turn right in front of the side door onto a footpath which crosses the lawn and reaches a junction.

Jaunting-car drivers traditionally ply their trade in a space to the right of the junction. Continue straight ahead there and follow signs for 'Dinish Cottage' and 'Meeting of the Waters'. The footpath crosses a large green lawn and is fringed by oak trees in places. On reaching a crossroads, veer left and follow signs for 'Colleen Bawn Rock' and 'Dinish Cottage'. The footpath soon forks in front of a private house. Veer left here, still following signs for 'Dinish Cottage' and pass a boathouse on the left.

You are now well away from the hustle and bustle of the Muckross House grounds. The footpath now winds along the northern end of Muckross Lake toward

Muckross Lake from Brickeen Bridge, with Eagles Nest behind.

Brickeen, and mostly under the canopy of trees. Torc Mountain appears on the left through a gap in the trees. On reaching a fork by the Reenadinna Wood board, veer left to pass the ruins of a stone-wall gated entrance. Reenadinna Wood is the largest area of yew woodland in Western Europe and the yew trees here are up to 250 years old.

As the footpath starts to rise and bend, the waters of Doo Lough can just about be seen across the greenery to the right, and Shehy Mountain rises majestically ahead. The footpath eventually passes a wooden bench on the left at **V 952**38 **858**79. Leave the footpath here momentarily and follow a sandy path through gorse and bracken to arrive at the shoreline of Muckross Lake, revealing fine views across to Torc Mountain.

Regain the footpath and continue for just under 200m before veering left once again to drop onto the sandy shore of the lake near Victoria Point. The Colleen Bawn Rock sits in the waters just ahead, framed by Eagles Nest and a backdrop of hills including Shehy and Torc Mountains. The famed rock was named after a 1911 black-and-white silent film, *The Colleen Bawn,* which was shot here and in the surrounding area.

Having enjoyed the views, continue again on the footpath toward Dinish Cottage. After a bend, Lough Leane can be seen through gaps in the trees and shrubs to the right. Look out also for the Prince of Wales Rock, a 26m (85ft) outcrop on the lake.

The footpath eventually reaches the concrete bridge at Brickeen, where contrasting views unfold in opposite directions. To the south, the rugged profile of Eagles Nest forms the backdrop behind a reed-filled section of the lake. To the north, the waters of Muckross drain out into Glena Bay, one of the many bays that give Lough Leane its shape. The small outline of Derby's Garden, one of the many islands and islets on its vast waters, can be seen ahead where the foothills of Shehy Mountain meet the lake.

Continue ahead to reach a multiway junction by a slipway on the left, with picnic tables, Dinish Cottage and its tearooms on the right. The 18th-century cottage was built by the Herberts and used as a hunting lodge and woodcutter's hut. The Meeting of the Waters is around 100m to the right. Follow signs from the cottage along a narrow path that veers left of the toilets to reach a clearing where the Old Weir Bridge is visible at the far end of a channel of water. The bridge is the gateway to the Meeting of the Waters where the three Killarney lakes – Lough Leane, Muckross Lake and the Upper Lake (via the Long Range) – converge.

Retrace steps back to the slipway and veer right there following signs for 'Exit to N71 1.6km'. Cross a wooden footbridge soon after and follow the footpath with Torc Mountain rising directly ahead. You are now on the southern end of Muckross Lake and the footpath soon passes Bog Bay on the left, with Shehy Mountain in the background. A bed of reeds in Bog Bay rustle in the wind.

The footpath undulates under the cover of trees to reach a car park by the N71. Veer right and cross the road to meet a walking trail to Torc Waterfall and Muckross House, marked by yellow, blue and red arrows. The trail goes up a slight rise then levels and passes some stone steps rising on the right. Ignore this and continue ahead, following the yellow and blue arrows. The trail undulates under the trees above the noisy N71, giving occasional glimpses toward the northern fringes of Muckross Lake through gaps in the rhododendron thickets and trees.

The trail eventually meets the N71 again. Cross the road with care and drop into an earthen track at the rear of the car park. Veer right along the track, following signs for 'Muckross House'. The track forks at the gateway of a large house on the right. Take a left there and cross a concrete bridge to reach a T-junction.

Here you are on tarmac once again. Turn left and follow signs for 'Muckross House 1.7km'. The footpath runs across a large green meadow bordered by electric fences. There are fine views of Shehy and Purple Mountains on the left and Torc Mountain behind. When the footpath forks, veer left and go through iron gates to follow a path close to the lakeshore. The footpath meanders under a canopy of trees and passes Dundag Boat

Muckross House.

House on the left, where boat trips out to Dinish Cottage are popular with tourists.

Continue along the footpath, ignoring all side paths until emerging out of the cover of trees. Muckross House can be seen in all its glory across a green lawn soon after. Turn right on a footpath toward the House and retrace steps back to the start.

Old Kenmare Road

Galway's Bridge to Kenmare		Torc Waterfall to Kenmare	
Grade:	1	Grade:	2
Distance:	10.5km (6½ miles)	Distance:	18.5km (11½ miles)
Ascent:	250m (820ft)	Ascent:	490m (1,608ft)
Time:	3–4 hours	Time:	5½–7 hours

Map:	OSi 1:50,000 Sheet 78, OSi 1:25,000 Adventure Series *MacGillycuddy's Reeks & Killarney National Park* or Harvey Superwalker 1:30,000 *MacGillycuddy's Reeks & Killarney National Park*

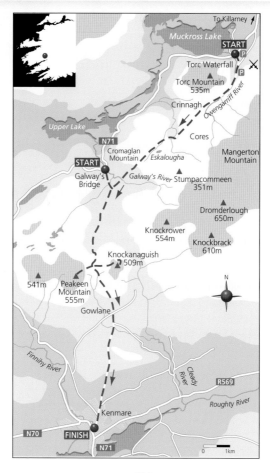

The Old Kenmare Road was an old thoroughfare linking the settlements of Kenmare and Killarney up to a period in the mid-19th century. It was then, during the Clearances, that bridges along the old road were destroyed to prevent public passage. Native Irish people living along the road were evicted from their homes by landlords who wanted the land for deer hunting or development of estates. Today, this old road is part of the Kerry Way, which forms a Y-junction at a point just south of Galway's Bridge. This route traces two variants of the Old Kenmare Road to Kenmare town: one from Galway's Bridge, and a longer variant from Torc Waterfall or Cloghereen Upper.

Galway's Bridge to Kenmare

Start: Coming from Killarney, use the car park on the left after Galway's Bridge by Derrycunnihy Church at **V 913**90 **802**78.
Finish: Kenmare town. Alternatively, there is a lay-by with spaces for two cars where the Kerry Way meets the road at Gowlane at **V 917**38 **751**80. This will avoid the road-walk of nearly 4.5km (2¾ miles) toward the end.

Route Description

Derrycunnihy Church was built in the 19th century reputedly to the design of the English architect Augustus Pugin. The church served the community living in the Black Valley at the time, who used to walk the 6km or so around the southern shores of the Upper Lake each Sunday for Mass.

Church by Galway's Bridge and Kerry Way signposts.

From the car park, with the church on the right, take the right fork before the bridge on to a boreen signposted 'Kerry Way to Killarney' and 'Kerry Way to Kenmare'. Follow the boreen around several bends. When it straightens, there is grassy moorland on either side with the rugged hillside of Incheens farther away. After several hundred metres, pass a junction and footpath on the left signposted 'Kerry Way to Killarney' at **V 916**13 **797**47.

Ignore the junction and continue straight ahead. The conical shape of Peakeen Mountain can be seen rising prominently ahead, with the flatter top of Knockanaguish to its left. The boreen is fringed with tormentil and tussocky grass, and clumps of wild rhododendron invade the rugged landscape. The Incheens valley is full of birdsong, and a deer fence runs by the woodlands to the left. The deer-fencing project is a restoration

Last light falls behind Peakeen Mountain, as seen from Knockanaguish.

strategy for the native woodlands in Killarney National Park. The lack of regeneration of flora within these woodlands is due to invasive species of rhododendron and grazing pressure from deer, feral goats and sheep. The deer fence houses separate enclosures with corridors for shelter and movement of deer through the woodlands, and will be removed once significant regeneration of woodlands has occurred.

Pass a junction on the right with a large house at the end. Continue ahead there as the boreen reduces to a track. After a lay-by on the left, the track rises then dips to a stream. Cross the stream, using stepping stones if necessary. Cross a larger stream around 100m further where there are stepping boulders with a rope-rail for support. This is followed by a smaller stream just after.

The track becomes stony and rocky and is fringed with bracken, rhododendron, butterwort, gorse and tormentil. A stream rumbles to the left. The landscape away from the track is wild and desolate, with erratics, grassy knolls and rocky outcrops of various shapes and sizes for company. The track gradually rises to a copse of trees on the right at **V 912**22 **784**10 where feral goats are common. There is a ruined building flanked by a mossy stone wall up the sheltered slope behind the trees.

Continue along the track southward and cross occasional streams. The track rises gradually uphill following a fence on the left to reach a large slab of rock on the col between Peakeen Mountain and Knockanaguish at **V 909**62 **768**71. It is a fine viewpoint to appreciate the wild and barren landscape, especially to the north. The call of sheep can be heard echoing at the best of times.

Peakeen Mountain/Knockanaguish extension: From the col between Peakeen Mountain and Knockanaguish, it is possible to ascend either summit (or both!). For **Peakeen Mountain**, ascend the spur westward and later veer south-westward to reach the trig point on the compact summit. Avoid the cliffs and crags by keeping on the northern side of Peakeen and bypass any rock benches by using grassy and rocky ramps. Descend the way you came. Add an additional distance of 1.5km (1 mile), 230m (755ft) ascent and 1–1¼ hours' walking time for this Grade 3 extension.

For **Knockanaguish**, head eastward from the col and aim for the tiny Lough Nagannee around 700m away. Pass the lake on the left and under steep ground and gullies that guard the western flanks of Knockanaguish. Contour briefly along the hillside then rise gradually until in line with the spur on the northern end of Knockanaguish. Veer southward there and ascend the spur for around 200m to reach the summit knoll. Descend the way you came. Add an additional distance of 3km (1¾ miles), 180m (591ft) ascent and 1¼–1¾ hours' walking time for this Grade 3 extension.

Descend on the track on the opposite side of the col and continue south towards Kenmare. The ground undulates after passing a patch of forestry on the right, often filled with the call of the cuckoo from May to July. Wire-meshed sleepers have been installed to prevent further erosion along sections of the track. As the end of the forestry is reached, Kenmare Sound comes into view and so do the hills of Beara and west Cork in the distance.

Continue to descend along the track to meet a road junction at **V 917**₃₈ **751**₈₀ in the townland of Gowlane. Continue ahead here for Kenmare town, which is around 4.5km away. Follow Kerry Way signposts along the road as it meanders under the cover of trees and passes wide grassy plains, turning back occasionally for views of Peakeen and the rest of the hills behind.

Pass some houses after around 2km and then the Kilmurry Business Technology Park, Kenmare Innovation Centre and the Kenmare Salmon Company, a white building with large blue doors. The road improves from here as it leads toward Kenmare town. Pass Kenmare Shopping Centre on the left and a school on the right followed by Willow Lodge B&B, a car park and a church before reaching Kenmare town. A place where land and sea meet in harmony, Kenmare is reflected in its contrasting Irish names: *An Neidín*, the 'little nest', which is a reference to the town set among the hills, and the newer name of *Ceann na Mara*, the 'head of the sea'.

Torc Waterfall to Kenmare

Start: Drive along the N71 from Killarney toward Kenmare and pass the main gates for Killarney National Park and Muckross House on the right. After another 1.7km (1 mile) or so further, park at the Torc Waterfall car park on the left at **V 965**₇₇ **847**₈₂. You may also use the car park at Cloghereen Upper at **V 967**₀₀ **842**₃₀. However, doing so means omitting Torc Waterfall from the itinerary.
Finish: As per the 'Galway's Bridge to Kenmare' route.

Route Description

The initial part of the route from Torc Waterfall, up to Cloghereen Upper and to the start of the boardwalk at the base on the southern flanks of Torc Mountain is described in detail in Route 25. You may wish to include an extension and ascend Torc Mountain. If not, continue along the Old Kenmare Road toward Esknamucky Glen.

The Old Kenmare Road soon passes below the northern slopes of Cores Hill at Crinnagh. Place names on the hillside here provide clues to a hidden past. Inchabalinmo (*Inse Baile na mBó*, 'water meadow of the town of the cows') suggests an old booley site for cattle. Friars Glen and Davy's Fields are other signs of human occupancy. Some walls and ruined buildings scar the landscape, remnants of the mid-19th-century Clearances.

Holy Cross Church, Kenmare

The trail here is also part of the Kerry Way. It descends to cross the Crinnagh River across a boggy area. There are sections of boardwalk to prevent further erosion. The trail passes the small lake of Eskalougha on the left then rises uphill through Esknamucky Glen between the slopes of Cromaglan Mountain and Stumpacommeen. A dense oak forest is soon reached and trail crosses the Galway River to eventually meet the junction at **V 916**₁₃ **797**₄₇. Turn left at the junction and follow the route as described in the 'Galway's Bridge to Kenmare' route.

ROUTE 28:

Mangerton Mountain and Stoompa

Spectacular lake-filled, steep-sided glacial corries and breathtaking views of the Reeks and Lough Leane – what more could one ask for?

Normal Route	
Grade:	3
Distance:	9.5km (6 miles)
Ascent:	760m (2,493ft)
Time:	3¾–4½ hours
Map:	OSi 1:50,000 Sheet 78, OSi 1:25,000 Adventure Series *MacGillycuddy's Reeks & Killarney National Park* or Harvey Superwalker 1:30,000 *MacGillycuddy's Reeks & Killarney National Park*

Stoompa Variation	
Grade:	4
Distance:	14.5km (9 miles)
Ascent:	960m (3,150ft)
Time:	5¼–6½ hours
Map:	OSi 1:50,000 Sheet 78, OSi 1:25,000 Adventure Series *MacGillycuddy's Reeks & Killarney National Park* or Harvey Superwalker 1:30,000 *MacGillycuddy's Reeks & Killarney National Park* AND OSi 1:50,000 Sheet 79

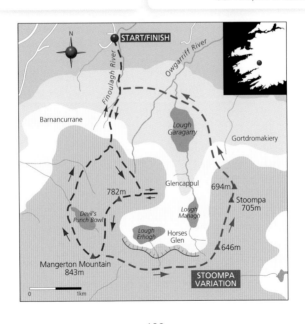

Start/finish: Drive along the N71 toward Kenmare from Killarney town. After just over 4km (2.5 miles), turn left into a minor road signposted 'Mangerton'. Follow the road for just under 2km (1¼ miles) to reach a junction. Turn right there and continue for another 2km (1¼ miles) to park near the 'Going Climbing' signboard at **V 983**₉₅ **848**₃₀.

Note: The walk grade of 3 is given due to the navigation skills required on Mangerton's broad expanse, and the trackless ground to the edge of the spur above Glencappul. Otherwise the walk is on a decent path, and should pose no problems for the beginner hillwalker. For the Stoompa Variation, the outflow of Lough Garagarry and the Owgarriff River may be difficult to cross on a wet day.

The Mangerton massif is one of the largest areas of desolate mountain wilderness in south-west Ireland. Its southernmost slopes form a broad plateau with miles of brown moorland where herds of deer can frequently be seen. This walk briefly takes us on this plateau to the summit of Mangerton Mountain (843m/2,766ft). However, the main attraction is away from its summit – along its ridge and the edge of its spurs where deep hollows are carved in its steep northern flanks. Here, distant views of the MacGillycuddy's Reeks and the mountains of Iveragh are spellbinding, especially on a clear evening when the sun dips down behind those peaks.

Ascending Mangerton's northern slopes with the Devil's Punch Bowl in the background.

Route Description

There is a board on 'Going Climbing and Country Code' and a sign for 'Mangerton Self Catering Accommodation' near the parking area. A path once used as a pony route for tourists runs uphill from here. Cross a tarmac bridge over the Finoulagh River and go up a stony path littered with gorse and bracken to a metal gate at **V 985**₂₈ **842**₀₂. A river flows in a gorge to the left. The path continues past clumps of bracken and then crosses a stream after a distance of about 150m. It passes near the site of Tooreencormick Battle Field. In 1262, the McCarthys, the ruling men of south Munster, fought the invading Normans in a bloody battle. The McCarthys ultimately defeated the Normans; however, the brother of their leader, Cormac McCarthy Reagh, was killed in the attack. And henceforth the area was known as *Tuairín Cormaic*, or the 'little field of Cormac'.

The path, the sides of which are covered in heather, goes up the hillside gradually. A stream tumbles across boulders on the right. After a distance of just over a kilometre uphill, you will pass three rocky cairns. At the third cairn at **V 982**85 **828**11, leave the main path and follow a faint track to the left.

Ascend south-eastward up moderate slopes for nearly a kilometre, aiming for the col east of summit 782m. The faint path almost disappears altogether as you ascend the grassy and heathery slope toward the col. On reaching the col at **V 989**31 **819**28, there is a fenced-off area. Go up a slight rise beyond it to the east, and then drop down to the top of the spur at **V 992**31 **819**68 to gaze down at the awesome depths of Glencappul and the Horses Glen below: Lough Erhogh in its deepest western reaches, Lough Managh to the east, and both of these surrounded by cliffs flanking the Mangerton massif and the heights of Stoompa. Lough Garagarry guards the entrance to this remote corner further north.

Go back up the rise, then down to a col, and finally up westward slopes leading to point 782m. Descend from here to a grassy and stony track that becomes increasingly rocky. Follow the ridge, with the steep drop and Lough Erhogh on your left and the Devil's Punch Bowl on your right, as it veers southward. As you ascend the slopes to a cairn at the rim of the Mangerton plateau at **V 982**03 **810**64, views down into the Devil's Punch Bowl become more impressive. In days of yore, a monster was said to have been banished by a holy saint into this watery prison for eternity.

From the cairn, head south-westward on a grid bearing of 210º (adjust for magnetic variation appropriately) and for a distance of 350m to the summit of Mangerton, taking extra care along the broad plateau in the mist. There is a trig point on the summit at **V 980**32 **807**88 and also a silver metal box and a windswept mast. Stone markers on the ground labelled N, S and W point in the direction of these three cardinal points of the compass.

Enchanting evening light envelops Mangerton's summit ridge above the Horses Glen.

The word 'BLARNEY' is also spelt on the ground with stones.

From Mangerton's summit, descend north-westward for a distance of 600m and a bearing of 316º (adjust for magnetic variation appropriately) to a metal post at **V 976**33 **812**03. Here, with breathtaking views of the distant MacGillycuddy's

Looking across Glencappul to Stoompa, with Lough Guitane in the background. Lough Garagarry is to the left, and the descent route from Stoompa to its outflow in the far left can be seen.

Reeks, the Iveragh mountains and Lough Leane below, descend the spur northward. With the Devil's Punch Bowl below on your right, follow the edge of the plateau to reach the mouth of the lake where a stream flows away from it at **V 975**52 **817**28. Cross the stream and follow the stony path which leads you back to the three cairns you encountered earlier in the day.

From here, simply retrace your steps back to the start point.

Stoompa Variation

Cross the tarmac bridge over the Finoulagh River and follow the route description from the car park near the 'Going Climbing' signboard to the summit of Mangerton Mountain as described in the Normal Route.

From the summit of Mangerton, descend eastward on moorland. The ground is relatively benign for 1km or so. Veer left toward the clifftop above the Horses Glen but keep a safe distance from the edge at all times. Now, with the steep drop on your left, descend eastward following the clifftop. Later, veer northward over point 646m and then ascend the slopes to the summit cairn of Stoompa at **W 006**48 **817**82.

The summit of Stoompa provides spectacular views down into the glacial corries housing Lough Erhogh, Lough Managh and Loch Garagarry and across to the cliffs at the back wall of the Horses Glen and Glencappul. In the opposite direction to the east, Crohane rises majestically, and farther away The Paps greet the horizon.

Descend northward from Stoompa toward point 694m, then veer left (north-westward) and descend the rough, steep spur to the northern end of Lough Garagarry. Cross the outflow of the lake and follow an intermittent path northward for around 300m to finally cross the Owgarriff River.

Set a course west after crossing the river and contour along the rough, heathery hillside for around 900m to rejoin main (Devil's Punch Bowl) track near **V 984**80 **839**00. Turn right on the track and follow it back to the start.

ROUTE 29:
Bennaunmore and Crohane

A challenging route over two rugged summits above Lough Guitane via a beautiful wooded valley.

Grade:	4
Distance:	16km (10 miles)
Ascent:	800m (2,625ft)
Time:	6–7½ hours, time added for difficulty of terrain
Map:	OSi 1:50,000 Sheet 79

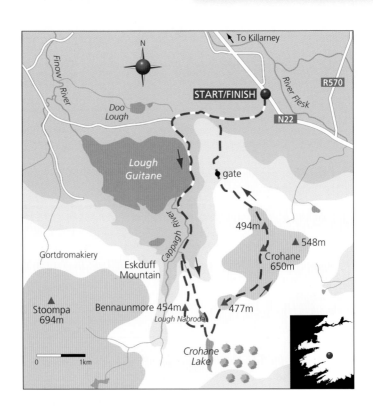

Start/finish: From Killarney, drive toward the N72/N22 junction. Around 6.5km (4 miles) after this junction, leave the N22 before Glenflesk and turn right along a narrow road. Reach a school shortly after and park there at **W 051**₇₇ **860**₃₈. Note that the 'traditional' parking lay-by to the east of Lough Guitane is no longer advised as the boreen leading to it is now severely potholed. There are some parking spaces along the minor road between the Artists' Gallery and the Lough Guitane junction at Rossalia which would reduce the road-walk at the start – but this is at the front wall of houses so seek permission before parking.

This route visits the summits of Bennaunmore (454m/1,489ft) and Crohane (650m/2,133ft) via the beautiful wooded gully near Cappagh Glen. It approaches Cappagh Glen along the shores of the wonderfully scenic Lough Guitane. The gully leads to a quiet, narrow upper valley flanked by steep cliffs. Two remote mountain lakes are visited en route to the two summits, both affording commanding views of the timeless Iveragh landscape.

The narrow V-shaped valley on the eastern flanks of Bennaunmore, with Lough Guitane beyond.

Route description

Walk southwards towards a T-junction around 100m away from the school. Turn right there and follow the minor road for around 2.2km towards Lough Guitane. Pass the Artists' Gallery followed by a house with a Marian statue, and a farmhouse on the right. The road then dips and passes some houses on the right. There is a metal gate by a white wall opposite the third house on the right (and just before a bend) at **W 032**₀₆ **856**₈₈. Turn left into a narrow lane there.

Continue for around 600m to reach a house on the right and go through a metal gate to its left. The lane bends right at the end of a small field and leads downhill under a cover of trees. The next 2km or so are a delightful stretch near the lakeshore of Lough Guitane. A string of mountains, including Stoompa and as far as the Reeks, forms a backdrop.

The lane is severely potholed and unmaintained. In a few hundred metres, you will pass the 'traditional' parking spot at a lay-by on the left at **W 036**₂₆ **846**₉₃. At the end of the road there is a metal gate with a sign 'Notice to all walkers: no dogs allowed beyond this point.' Go through this gate and pass a house and building on the left followed by another metal gate.

Lough Nabroda and Crohane Lake from the summit slopes of Bennaunmore.

Follow a track across a flat grassy area until it forks. The right fork crosses a concrete bridge toward a brick house and the left leads toward some trees and mountains ahead. Take the left option here to reach a metal gate. The track soon reduces to a path as it leads through a wooded area with the Cappagh River flowing to the right. The path runs through a field with a zinc-roofed building on the left and metal gates on either end.

The path crosses a stream on the right and then heads toward open mountainside with Bennaunmore rising ahead to the left with Stoompa to its right. Soon, take a right at a fork at **W 035**69 **832**79 and cross another stream after. The path then meanders along the bracken-covered ground to reach another fork around 300m away at the base of Bennaunmore. Here you may choose to either ascend a wooded gully on the left or tackle Bennaunmore head-on to the right.

For variety of scenery and interest, it is recommended to take the left fork and ascend the wooded gully to reach a V-shaped valley above. Follow a stream on the left initially before the intermittent path leads steeply up the woods. Some fallen branches and trunks have to be crossed and the moss-covered rocks are slippery when wet, so take care.

This is a delightful stretch. The path turns rocky beyond the woods and is flanked by steeper slopes laced with bracken, heather, rhododendron and rocky crags. When the slope begins to relent, steal a glance back to the gap in the 'V' with Lough Guitane framed by cliffs on either side. The path then undulates along the V-shaped valley for a few hundred metres to reach Lough Nabroda at **W 037**79 **819**20.

Lough Nabroda is housed in a hollow at the base of steep cliffs in a remote setting. A set of vertical rock columns towers above a boulder field to the right. With the lake to the right, follow a path by its shoreline to reach its far (southern) end.

Veer right here and follow an intermittent, grassy and rocky path uphill toward the saddle of a broad ridge. Crohane Lake and some wind farms come into view to the south as height is gained. Turn right on the ridge and continue until reaching the summit of Bennaunmore at **W 035**₀₆ **819**₅₀, marked by some small rocks nested amongst the grass and heather. There is a stunning view down to Cappagh Glen, flanked by Eskduff Mountain and Crohane, and with Lough Nabrean and Lough Guitane directly ahead.

From the summit, retrace steps back down the slope to the southern end of Loch Nabroda. From there, veer right and walk on flat, grassy and tussocky ground to reach Crohane Lake. The lake is an oasis of heather, shrubs and trees and is rocky on its eastern end. Pick a vague path to the left (eastern end) of the lake and ascend the ground there.

Once above the lake, veer north/north-east and ascend the spur toward point 439m and point 477m. The lower slope is overgrown with tussocky grass and heather besides the grass and rock. Descend to a complex col after point 477m to meet a fence at **W 045**₆₉ **822**₂₀. Follow the fence uphill for around 400m until the ground flattens, then cross it and veer left (northward) toward Crohane.

Although steep, the slope is mainly on short heather and grass with scattered rock. There is a cairn and a small battery-powered antenna on the summit of Crohane (*An Cruachán*, 'the little stack'). The summit provides commanding 360-degree views of the surrounding area that encompasses Crohane Lake, Bennaunmore, Stoompa, Mangerton, a host of distant Iveragh peaks, the MacGillycuddy's Reeks, Purple and Tomies Mountains, Lough Leane, Lough Guitane, the plains of Killarney, the Paps and nearly all the hills of west Cork and Beara.

Make sure the correct spur is taken on the descent, particularly in the mist – aim to descend north-west toward Shronaboy. Keeping Lough Guitane ahead to the left, descend a grassy slope with scattered rocks to reach a flat grassy area just before point 458m. Follow a fence down the slope to reach another fence running perpendicular to it. Cross this fence and shortly after veer away from it and descend the steep, grassy and heathery spur until a track below comes into view.

This is the track you need to aim for at Shronaboy. Veer left (westward) at point 348m to position yourself just above the track at **W 043**₁₃ **843**₀₆. By doing so, you are avoiding an area of steep, rocky, uneven, bracken and heather covered ground directly to the north. From **W 043**₁₃ **843**₀₆, descend through bracken and grassy patches toward the track below and reach a metal gate at **W 041**₉₇ **846**₃₁.

The view toward Lough Guitane from the summit of Crohane.

The gate leads to an enclosed area with a small concrete hut and another gate on its far end. Do not enter the enclosure but use a small, rusted metal gate on the right to bypass it. Follow a track beyond, going through two more metal gates before passing a farmhouse on the left. The track soon becomes a tarmac lane and passes a house on the right. The lane leads downhill and back to the minor road at the start. Turn right and walk along the road back to the car park by the school.